Recreational Games and Tournaments

Acknowledgements

We wish to thank the following organisations or persons for their help and support in preparing this book:

- Publication Fund for Physical Education (Publicatiefonds voor Lichamelijke Opvoeding, vzw - Flanders, Belgium) in allowing us to translate the original work "Organisatie van sportieve evenementen. Sportdagen - Recreatieve club-tornooien - Recreatiesportevenementen" from Dutch to English and providing us with a number of pictures
- The company Marny for their permission in using some of their pictures
- Sebastien Godfroid and Randy Rzewnicki for helping with the translation
- Linda Bogemans for her administrative work
- Jos Theeboom for making some of the pictures

De Knop/Theeboom/Van Puymbroeck/De Martelaer/Wittock

Recreational Games and Tournaments

The organisation of small- and intermediate-sized events

Meyer & Meyer Verlag

Original title: „Organisatie van sportieve evenementen"
© Publicatiefonds voor Lichamelijke Opvoeding vzw 1995
Editor: vzw P.V.L.O., W. Verbessem, Gent

Die Deutsche Bibliothek – CIP-Einheitsaufnahme

Recreational games and tournaments :
the organisation of small- and intermediate- sized events / Paul De Knop ... u.a.
- Aachen : Meyer und Meyer, 1998
ISBN 3-89124-446-0

© 1998 by Meyer & Meyer Verlag, Aachen
Cover photo: Bongarts Sportfotografie GmbH, Hamburg
Photos and illustration: Paul De Knop, Publication Fund for Physical Education,
Jos Theeboom, Marny
Cover design: Walter J. Neumann, N & N Design-Studio, Aachen
Editorial: Jo-Anne Cox, Tremorfa (Cardiff); Dr. Irmgard Jaeger, Aachen
Cover exposure: frw, Reiner Wahlen, Aachen
Exposure: frw, Reiner Wahlen, Aachen
Printed by Röder + Moll GmbH, Mönchengladbach
Printed in Germany
ISBN 3-89124-446-0

Table of Contents

Introduction

In recent years there has been a growing interest in the organisation of or partici-pation in big, as well as, small sports events. These events are being organised in clubs, schools, municipalities, youth centres, corporate world, etc. However, the realisation and organisation of these kinds of events requires a lot of hard work.

This book tries to be an aid for all those who are either professionally or volun-tarily involved in the organisation of sports events. This includes, among others, physical education teachers, people responsible for the guidance of school sports activities, municipal sports services, physical education student-teachers and recreational sports leaders.

The book consists of two parts. The **first part** describes a step-by-step approach for the **organisation** of a small- to intermediate-sized event. This "theoretical" information is supported with examples of intermediate-sized events. The **second part** consists of examples of small events, with an emphasis on the **content** of these events.

The events that are described in this book are examples from recreational sport which can be altered according to the available accommodation, time, creativity of the organisers, target group for which the event is organised, etc.

As a reader one should understand that not all possible sports events can be described here. For practical reasons a selection has been made. However, this book contains enough elements to organise numerous (school) sports days, recreational club tournaments and recreational sports events.

Why choose recreational sport?

Recreational sport can be described as **a form of sport in which everybody can participate in their own way**. The emphasis is on enjoyment, recreation, self-realisation and social contact. This does not mean, however, that competitive sport should be rejected, while recreational sport is being idealised. It is our belief that recreational sport only reaches its full potential if it is **functionally** as well as **supplementarily** related to competitive sport. In other words, children and adults must be able to get in touch with competitive sport through recreational sport, because the tight organisation and severe standards of competitive sport often make it very difficult for beginners to become involved.

This is, however, not the only aim of recreational sport. On the contrary, recrea-tional sport should also be directed towards a life-time participation for all. Elite and competitive sport are only accessible for a small minority and, moreover, for a limited period in their life. Therefore, recreational sport is also aimed at the under-privileged and can offer a life-time involvement for all.

If recreational sport is **functionally related** to (competitive) sport, it means that:
1. Recreational sport should remain sport and can never be merely play.
2. Recreational sport can not oppose competitive sport as it might be, in some cases, an introduction to competitive sport.
3. Performance should not be banned from recreational sport. However, on the one hand, to develop optimally, recreational sport should be freed from the "urge to achieve at all costs" which is a characteristic of elite sport. On the other hand, if no element of achievement is present in recreational sport, one can hardly speak of sport at all. Therefore, recreational sport must also include performance, but it should not be imposed upon the players.
4. The term "recreational sport" is partly related to the way sport is practised, but not solely.

If recreational sport is **supplementarily related** to (competitive) sport, it means that:
1. Recreational sport, as well as competitive sport, can be regarded as a type of sport. Recreational sport however, is a sport played for entertainment and relaxation. From the moment sport is no longer played solely for recreational purposes, but (also) for other reasons, one can not speak of recreational sport, but rather of professional sport, therapy, etc.
2. Recreational sport is different from competitive sport in that the former is directed towards all people (children, adults, retired people, handicapped, etc) and towards life-time involvement.
3. Recreational sport requires a very specific organisation and a totally different approach:
   a. Recreational sport requires a more democratic type of leadership as opposed to the often authoritarian approach in competitive sport.
   b. In recreational sport the method of practising is adjusted according to the level of the participants. In competitive sport on the other hand, participants need to adjust to the existing rules and standards.
   c. In recreational sport a lot of attention is paid to the appreciation of others: participants are encouraged to view opponents as partners knowing that without the presence of each other, there is no sport.
   d. Recreational sport contributes more significantly to social contact than competitive sport, as a recreational sports participant can only play in relation to the other or the group. Social contact is also very important for the continuing character of recreational sports practice.
   e. Recreational sport is more directed towards variation than towards specialisation (the latter being an unconditional necessity in competitive sport). The wide variety of activities creates the possibility of fulfilling the individual needs of all participants. By not limiting oneself to the internationally recognized

sports rules, the possibility of different choices increases so that everyone can find what they personally are looking for. Once they follow a certain path, recreational sports participants often also end up in a sort of specialisation, but without being driven to it by a compelling need.

Based on the above mentioned facts, it can be stated that recreational sport and competitive sport are both a part of the bigger entity **sport**. One can therefore state that they are intertwined.

As mentioned before, recreational sport should be regarded as a full-bodied form of sport. The division of sport into recreational sport and competitive sport means that the two elements are emphasised differently. While the "recreational" element is being stressed in recreational sport, the "achievement" element receives full attention in competitive sport.

Talking about recreational sport is, in our opinion, almost impossible because it is a sports form that must be permanently adjusted to the changing needs and wishes of participants. As it is not really the content that counts, but more a mental state (sociability, life-time involvement, limited performance orientation, etc.) and because there is a specific organisation and approach (heterogeneous groups, no strings attached, continuity, etc.), we personally prefer to talk about **"recreational sports practice"** instead of "recreational sport". Throughout this book, we hope to stress that it is the way in which sport takes place which determines if one will talk about "recreational sport", or rather, "recreational sports practice".

Why choose recreational organisation forms?

If one refers to organisational forms in a sports context, one often thinks about traditional competition forms, such as the competition system in soccer or the "knock-out" system in tennis. The games take place according to a tight organisational structure and fixed rules. The attention primarily goes to the winner of the competition season or the tournament. Only the best are rewarded.

Parallel to these traditional organisational forms, recreational types of organisation can be offered. These are directed towards a larger audience. They are open to everyone, without regard to age, gender or skill level and there are more possibilities in variation and organisation. This can be a way to attract more people (again) to sport. As these types of organisation are not commonly used in a sports context, we feel that this book can be used as a useful aid.

PART 1

THE ORGANISATION OF AN EVENT

To achieve a perfectly run sports event, well-thought out planning as well as good organisation are essential. In this section we will describe a step by step organisation plan for a small- to intermediate-sized event, with consideration to the available facilities, personnel and finances. It goes without saying that this is a general programme. It can be adapted according to the particular nature of the event.

Figure 1: The different phases in the realisation of an event

STARTING PHASE

formulate objectives
brainstorming with a project group
determine the basic lines of the project
determine the criteria for success

PLANNING PHASE

develop an action plan
determine the finances
conclude contracts/make agreements
search for and instruct co-workers
develop a scenario

IMPLEMENTATION PHASE

implement the event
solve unforeseen problems
clean up

EVALUATION PHASE

thank the staff and co-workers
evaluation of the event

1. Starting Phase

When a group decides to organise an event, a project group immediately has to be formed to work out the planning concretely.
(Because a large group decreases effectiveness and functionality, working with a small project group is recommended). Much depends on the qualities of the  leader, but a group of seven or eight people is perfect. If after a while you realise that you need more people to do the necessary tasks, you can always decide to form new subcommittees.

The planning period for a small- to intermediate-sized event is about one year. Tasks such as selecting the site, making contacts with possible sponsors and the development of a publicity plan take more time and must be done in advance.

It is evident that the organisation, together with the project group, has to think about the objectives they want to realise by organising the event. Then a brainstorming session with the members of the project group has to be organised. This is a creative process during which the members of the project group can bring forward all the possible ideas or activities, without deciding if it is possible to realise them or not.

The next step is to examine the suggestions in light of the goals of the organisation, the wishes and the expectations of the different groups to whom the activity will be directed and the financial limitations. For a recreational sports club, for instance, a top sports event would not be the best means to promote their sport among young people. First of all, the realisation of such an event would probably exceed the financial means of the club and it would not realise the objective "acquaintance with and promotion of the workings of the club". Moreover, this project is not specially directed towards young people. A free-for-all sports day introducing different sports, such as mountain biking, climbing and trampoline jumping, would be a much better initiative.

After considering these different aspects, the basic procedures of the event should be fixed. More to the point: it should be determined where and when the event will take place, toward which groups the organisation will direct its activities, the schedule and the different types of activities which will be offered.

Afterwards, the project group has to think about the financial means, the manpower and site necessary for this event. This means that answers to the following questions are needed:
- What are the estimated expenses?
- What is the estimated income?
- How many co-workers and/or staff are needed on the day of the event and how many for the preparation?
- Which external organisations must be contacted for co-operation? (e.g., the local government, the police, first aid organisations, etc.)
- Which site and which specific parts of it are needed?
- Is the site easily accessible and is there enough parking?

If these minimum criteria cannot be fulfilled for one reason or another, the event has to be cancelled or a different kind of event created. It is clear that such a decision must be made as quickly as possible.

2. Planning Phase

Within the project group, it has to be agreed who is responsible for which part of the organisation. The following functions should be assigned individually:
- the project leader
- a public relations manager
- a financial manager/treasurer
- a secretary
- an activities manager
- a sponsorship manager
- a personnel manager

After the assignment of the different functions to the members of the project group, they each should make up a chart containing all the tasks that must be completed in order to realise the event. It is also recommended that a chart with all the tasks in chronological order is made up, as well as the person responsible and the financial needs for each function, the equipment and material needed. The following checklist can be used as a guideline to check that you have not forgotten anything during the planning phase.

CHECKLIST

Planning:
- O target
- O target group
- O type of event
- O date + time
- O what to do if the event is cancelled

Start on time with the preparations. Pay attention to:

- O written agreements about co-workers and employees, site and equipment
- O permits (local government, police, owner, etc.)
- O domestic regulations
- O the layout of the field
- O pointing out the co-ordinator
- O time schedule
- O distribution of tasks

Aspects:

a) *target groups*:
- O young people
- O elderly
- O men
- O women
- O mixed
- O neighbourhood
- O associations/groups
- O family
- O etc.

b) *equipment*:
- O What do you have?
- O What must you borrow?
- O What must you buy?
- O megaphone
- O sound installation

c) *date and time*:
- O Is everybody available at that time?
- O Avoid overlapping with other activities

d) *finances*:

income:
- O participants
- O advertisement
- O sponsorship
- O subsides
- O etc.

expenditure:
- O compensation for leadership
- O accommodation/facilities
- O game equipment
- O advertising
- O souvenirs
- O sound installation
- O insurance
- O etc.

e) *care*:
- O transport
- O first aid/doctor
- O beverage/food
- O list of participants

f) presentation: O   opening/distribution/closing
                    O   souvenirs
                    O   slogan
                    O   pre-inscription
                    O   inform the neighbours
                    O   advertisement
                                        O   mouth to mouth
                                        O   stencil
                                        O   leaflet, pamphlets
                                        O   poster
                                        O   press (regional radio, news-
                                            papers, local newspapers,....)
                                        O   sound car
                                        O   music
                                        O   announcer
                    O   entrance tickets
                    O   central memo board
                    O   information stand
                    O   invitation of special guests
                    O   programme book:
                                        O   address + telephone
                                            details of the event
                                        O   organising committee
                                        O   slogan
                                        O   domestic objectives
                                        O   aims of the event
                                        O   time schedule
                                        O   division of the participants
                                        O   summery of the activities
                                        O   ground-plan
                                        O   costs of participation
                                        O   sponsoring

Afterwards: O   returning the equipment
                   O   debriefing
                   O   report
                   O   settlement of accounts
                   O   thank each of the co-workers

During the planning phase, the project group must meet regularly in order to check on how well the different tasks for the action plans have been realised and to look for solutions to sudden problems. Try at all times to keep an agenda and make sure all decisions are noted in a (short) report.

Depending on the financial needs, partly expressed by the action plan, the treasurer has to make an **estimation** of the total costs of the event. In the same way a prognosis of the expected income of each activity can be made. Even if these financial estimates are based on previous similar events, it remains a difficult and risky business. Therefore, an item called "unforeseen" costs (which makes up about 10% of the total costs) always has to be included in the budget. Because the organisation will probably make appeals for sponsorship and grants in order to meet costs, the development of a sponsorship plan and contacts with possible sponsors are very important tasks.

Once the financial plan is finished, initial agreements about the rental of the site can be made and equipment as well as insurance acquired. In order to avoid problems, try to obtain a written **contract** for each of your agreements with people outside your organisation.

The next important step in the preparation of the event is the recruitment and training of the **co-workers**. For without extra co-workers (e.g., for the reception desk and registration of the partici-pants, for the parking attendants) the event will not be a success. Try to de-termine in advance the number of coworkers you will need as well as the qualities they need to have and the tasks they will have to do. As soon as the co-workers have been recruited, a meeting has to be organised in order to give these people more information about the goals and organisation of the event as well as about their specific tasks and responsibilities.

Meanwhile, the project group will develop the **time schedule**. This is a detailed summary containing every-thing that will happen on the day of the event, from the putting up of the tents or information stands, to the activities during the event and cleaning up and putting away the equipment. It should also be mentioned in this schedule who is responsible for which task and where each activity takes place.

If all the steps of the planning phase are done properly, very little can fail (except of course the weather!).

3. Implementation Phase

Long before the event starts, the whole team has to be present at the site. Putting up the equipment and making the last preparations may take more time than one would expect. During the entire event, good **co-ordination** and **communication** between the different managers is very important. Each of the fellow workers has to know who is responsible for what and where to go when there are some special or general problems. For major problems, deliberation is needed and the project leader will have to make the final decision.

Another important task for the project leader is **supervising** the whole event. This person must see that everything is running smoothly, according to the timing and agreements mentioned in the schedule.

When the event is finished, the whole team comes together for a drink so they can give their first impressions about the event. After this, all the equipment which was used that day must be put away or returned to the owner. Make sure that all the co-workers finish their tasks at the end of the event. For after a hard day of work, the saying "many hands make light work" counts more than ever.

4. Evaluation Phase

Shortly after the event the members of the project group should meet to **evaluate** the event and deal with the financial affairs. First of all, the question "Did we realise the objectives and attain the expected target groups?" has to be answered. But also the planning process and the implementation of the event have to be evaluated critically, in order to avoid the same errors when the next event is organised.
Some criteria for the evaluation of the event are:
- number of participants
- participant turnover
- participants' satisfaction or enjoyment
- the attainment of the objectives.

During the evaluation process a difference can be made between product and process evaluation.

During a product evaluation (output evaluation) the focus lies mainly on the attainment of the objectives which were put forward:
- Were the objectives reached?
- Did the activities deliver what you expected from them?

On the other hand, in a process evaluation, the whole process underlying the attainment of the objectives is evaluated:
- Was the activity well prepared in advance?
- How did the activity proceed?
- Did the didactic measures (explanations, aids, feedback) have the expected results?

The information necessary for the evaluation can be obtained through:
- team discussion(s)
- observation (preferably participatory)
- feedback from participants
- comparison (with previous or other programmes).

A useful tool for the evaluation is the schedule of the event. For, based on this schedule, one can check if the objectives were attained, if the activity occurred as planned and if changes have to be made for another edition.

An evaluation form can be used for the evaluation. The first point on this form must be the pleasure or enjoyment factor. The question: "Did the participants enjoy themselves?" should be answered in the affirmative and if this is not the case, the activities will have to be changed.

Other points for attention are:
- Publicity: was the event promoted sufficiently, and to the right people?
- Programme: was the programme attractive and well constructed?
- Equipment: was there enough equipment and was it in good condition?
- Co-workers: did they fulfil expectations; were they enthusiastic; did they know their tasks; how was their contact with the group?
- Reception desk contact: were the participants greeted pleasantly; did they receive sufficient information about the activities; did they receive answers to all their questions?
- Creativity: were the games creative enough; was the programme original, etc?
- Safety: were all necessary precautions taken to make the event as safe as possible; was the equipment safe; were the activities safe enough, etc?
- Number of activities: was the number sufficient; were they well spread over the available time, etc?
- General organisation: were there any problems; were the problems solved within a reasonable time, etc?
- Organisation: how was the event organised?
- Site: was the site appropriate for the activity and was it properly used, etc?
- Equipment: was it well placed and used; who put it away, etc?
- Did the participants know where they had to go; what they had to do; how the activities were to proceed, etc?
- Time: was the time available for the different parts of the event sufficient; was there enough time for explanations and the activity itself?

Next is an example of an evaluation form. The members of the project group should evaluate the different points by means of a score ranging from "very good" to "bad". There is also the choice of writing down some remarks or comments about the different points.

EVALUATION FORM

Activity: Number of participants:
Date: Evaluation:

	very good	good	mediocre	insufficient	bad
pleasure:	O	O	O	O	O
remarks:........................					
publicity/ advertisement:	O	O	O	O	O
remarks:........................					
programme:	O	O	O	O	O
remarks:........................					
equipment:	O	O	O	O	O
remarks:........................					
guidance/ evaluation:	O	O	O	O	O
remarks:........................					
greeting/contact:	O	O	O	O	O
remarks:........................					
creativity:	O	O	O	O	O
remarks:........................					
safety:	O	O	O	O	O
remarks:........................					
number of activities:	O	O	O	O	O
remarks:........................					
gen. co-ordination:	O	O	O	O	O
remarks:........................					
organisation:	O	O	O	O	O
remarks:........................					
general appraisal:	O	O	O	O	O
remarks:........................					

In many events, the **co-workers** play an important role. The project group, which took the initiative of organising this event, has to remember to **thank** the many co-workers, for example with a drink, a present or a trip, or even a simple letter.

Also the sponsors or donors have to be thanked for their financial input. For this purpose, an evaluation report in which some information is given about the event, the number of participants and the press attention, is very useful.

A SPECIFIC EXAMPLE

THE ORGANISATION OF A SPORTS DAY

The manager of the sports hall "All-in-sport" wants to promote the availability of its facilities to the schools in the neighbourhood. In order to realise this objective, it was decided to organise a sports day for all of the nearby schools.[1]

1) Starting Phase

First Meeting (21/09)
- Formation of a project group: Paul, Helena, Marc, Kristine, Linda
- Gather data and develop the main frame of the event

    * *General description of the event:* a sports day for 6th year pupils in secondary schools in the municipality, including the following activities:
        - traditional events of a competitive nature,
        - recreational events and adventure sports,
        - individual tests (e. g., Eurofit: a number of physical tests to evaluate the fitness level) on a "come and go" basis,
        - information about sports options in the neighbourhood.

    * *Objectives of the event:*
        - to get the schools acquainted with the sports hall,
        - to stimulate young people to do sport and to continue doing it regularly.

    * *Where:* sports grounds of the "All-in-sport" sports hall

    * *When:* February

    * *Brainstorming about possible activities:* squash, baseball, soccer, basketball volleyball, gymnastics, triathlon, open swimming event, mountainbiking, power training, aerobics, orientation run, table tennis, Eurofittests.

This example is based on an actual sports day which was organised by the authors on February 12th 1995.

Second Meeting (07/10)
-   Event date: February 12th
-   Activities:

     * Morning:

	9:00 AM – 9:30 AM:	greeting + registration
	9:30 AM – 10:00 AM:	mass aerobics/mass warm up/ information about the schedule of the sports day
	10:00 AM – 12:00 PM:	volleyball gymnastics aerobics fitness training squash (initiation + tournament) table tennis (initiation + tourna-ment) triathlon basketball soccer walking tour Eurofit-tests

     * Afternoon:

	12:00 PM – 13.30 PM:	shower + lunch
	13:30 PM – 16.30 PM:	volleyball gymnastics fitness training squash (initiation + tournament) table tennis (initiation + tourna-ment) open swimming event mountain biking basketball soccer baseball walking tour Eurofit-tests
	16:45 PM – 17:00 PM:	awarding of prizes/finish

-   Capacity:

	volleyball:	64 pupils/hour
	gymnastics:	20 pupils/hour
	aerobics:	40 pupils/hour

fitness training:	20 pupils/hour
squash:	22 pupils/hour
table tennis:	50 pupils/hour
triathlon:	20 pupils/hour
basketball:	56 pupils/hour
soccer:	32 pupils/hour
baseball:	20 pupils/hour
walking tour:	30 pupils/hour
Eurofit-tests:	20 pupils/hour
mountain biking:	30 pupils/hour

total capacity/hour: about 450 pupils
maximum day capacity: 500 pupils

- Proposed budget:

expenses:		
	site rental	for free
	equipment rental	$ 900
	paper	165
	administration	165
	equipment	835
	expenses staff/co-workers	265
	unforeseen costs	335
	insurance	·for free
	total:	$ 2,665

income:		
	participant fees	$ 835
	prizes	330
	sponsorship: tickets for free beverages	835
	use of equipment	665
	total:	$ 2,665

- Co-workers:
  * "All-in-sport" sports hall personnel (2 secretaries, 5 sports teachers)
  * Faculty of Physical Education interns (25 students)
- Number of co-workers:

preparation:		5
day of the event:	reception desk/walking tour	2
	warming up/aerobics	2
	volleyball	2
	triathlon/swimming	4
	squash	2

fitness training	2
gymnastics	4
mountain biking	3
basketball	2
baseball	1
table tennis	2
soccer	1
emergency team	3
total:	30

–   Criteria of success: balanced budget
make our club available
sufficient pupils
sufficient co-workers
meals sponsored + leaflets printed

Notes:
– The sports site is owned by the municipality and can be used for free.
– Positive feedback from the teachers of the schools has been received.
– We have enough co-workers because the students of the Faculty of Physical Education will be enlisted. Therefore the event is feasible.

2) Planning Phase

Third meeting (14/10)
Division of functions among the members of the project group:

co-ordinator:	Linda
PR-manager:	Helena
activities manager:	Kristine
secretary:	Marc
financial manager:	Paul

Tasks for the co-ordinator:
– General co-ordination
– Preparing agenda for each meeting
– Follow up the group members' tasks.

Tasks for the PR-manager:
– Write letters to the dean of the Faculty of Physical Education in order to ask for the students' co-operation for the event

- Contact the cafeteria for tickets for free meals + practical arrangements
- Write to the schools and announce the sports day (enclose inscription form)
- Apply for and confirm the rental of equipment
- Develop an information brochure (for possible sponsors)
- Inform the teachers (about 2 weeks before the event) using an information brochure
- Thank sponsors and co-workers afterwards.

Tasks for the activities manager:
- Draw up the event schedule
- Determine for each activity the number of co-workers needed and the tasks they have to fulfil; appoint a manager for each activity; draw up regulations; make a list of necessary equipment and what equipment is already present and what should be rented; purchase a first aid kit
- Organise presentations for opening and closing the sports day
- Inform the co-workers and students
- Draw up a ground plan of the site and the activities.

Tasks for the secretary:
- Write reports of the different meetings
- Take care of the reception, including sign-posts, map, registration stand, information, etc.
- Draw up the scenario of the event
- Keep the registration forms filled-in by the participating schools
- Take out sports insurance.

Tasks for the financial manager:
- Draw up a detailed budget
- Maintain the accounts
- Keep the contracts/invoices
- Arrange payments.

Each of the project group members has to draw up a time schedule for the different tasks that have to be done. This schedule gives information about which tasks and activities have to be carried out, the starting and finishing times of each activity and the people as well as money or equipment needed. The co-ordinator draws up a time schedule as well as an agenda for each meeting of the project group.

Make sure all the tasks are carried out by the time allocated in the schedule.

General schedule sports day 12/02

Time	activity	personnel	equipment	site	remarks
7:30 AM – 9:00 AM	gathering and placement of equipment	*	*	*	* see detailed programme
9:00 AM – 9:30 AM	registration of teachers and participants, change clothes, guide participants to the hall	10 teachers + participating schools	2 tables, 4 chairs, information brochure, sign-posts, equipment for registration desk	entrance locker rooms sports hall	
9:30 AM – 9:50 AM	welcome speech + mass warm up	manager + co-ordinator + 2 teachers	stereo installation, microphone, megaphone, 1 platform in each sports hall	hall L 1, 2, 3: with music hall L 4, 5, 6: without music	
9:50 AM – 12:00 PM	sports activities	*	*	*	*see detailed programme
12:00 PM – 13:30 PM	meal	teachers + co-workers reception desk	sign with the name of the school	cafeteria	programme appears in the folder
13:30 PM – 16:30 PM	sports activities	*	*	*	*see detailed programme
16:30 PM – 16:45 PM	clean up the sports hall	co-workers sports activities	dustbins	sports hall	
16:45 PM – 17:00 PM	award prizes	manager	prizes, microphone	sports hall	
17:00 PM – 17:30 PM	remove equipment, thank each of the co-workers	all the co-workers	tickets for free beverages for the co-workers		

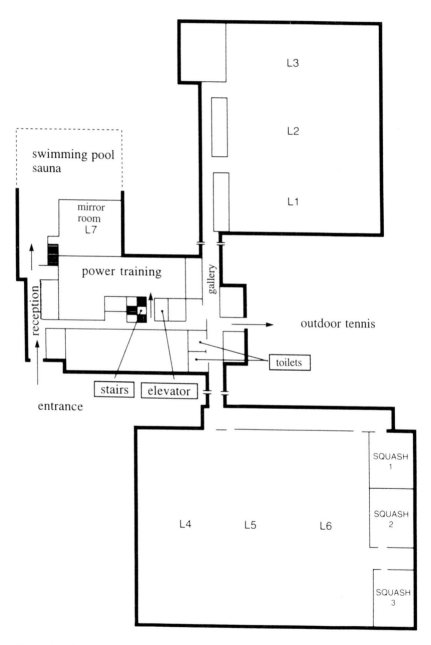

Floor plan for the accommodation

Fourth meeting (20/01)
Call all the different sports managers together and give a description of the tasks and some practical information such as:
- The number of co-workers during the day
- The rules of the competition(s)
- The list of equipment
- The placement of the equipment
- Draw up a schedule for the competitions
- Inform the co-ordinator about the first 3 places in the competition.

Fifth meeting (04/02)
The whole project group meets for the last time before the event. At this meeting the programme-scenario must be gone over carefully in order to see if all the tasks have been executed.

Sixth meeting (09/02)
Bring all the co-workers together for a last briefing of the programme as well as of the time schedule.

3) Detailed Programme

Mass warm up

Manager:	Janet	
Teachers:	Janet in L 1, 2, 3:	warm up to music
	Sigrid in L 4, 5, 6:	warm up without music
Teachers' tasks:	7:30 AM – 9:00 AM:	placement of the platform + stereo
	9:30 AM – 9:50 AM:	lead warm up
	9:50 AM:	remove the equipment after warming up
Equipment:	– stereo	
	– 2 platforms	

Volleyball

Manager:	Elly	
Location:	hall L2:	girls
	hall L3:	boys
Umpires:	Elly – Eric	
Scoreboard:	some of the extra players	
Co-workers' tasks:	9:50 AM:	placement of the equipment

10:00 AM – 12:00 PM:	lead the competition
13:30 AM – 16:30 PM:	lead the competition
16:30 AM:	remove the equipment
	pass the results on to the co-ordinator

Rules: The teams must be in the hall 10 minutes before the start of the competition. Each game takes 30 minutes (before the competition, a warm up of 10 minutes is possible).

Equipment:
- 2 volleyball nets + posts
- 20 volleyballs
- 2 scoreboards
- 2 umpire chairs
- paper + pencil
- 4 benches

Squash

Manager:	Kate
Location:	3 squash fields
Teacher of Initiation courses:	Ken
Scoreboard:	Kate
Co-workers' tasks:	9:50 AM:

make up competition programme (who plays against who? when? on which field?)

make up timetable for initiation courses

	10:00 AM – 12:00 PM:	teach initiation courses + keep up the scoreboard
	13:30 PM – 16:30 PM:	teach initiation courses + keep up the scoreboard
	16:30 PM:	removal of the equipment + pass the results on to the co-ordinator

Rules: Each game takes 20 minutes and the players themselves keep score. The players have to meet the squash manager at least 5 minutes before the starting time. A maximum of 10 participants per hour is allowed on the initiation courses.

Equipment: – 6 squash rackets
                  – 6 squash balls
                  – a large piece of paper
                  – a marker pen

Mini Triathlon

Manager:	Eve
Location:	swimming pool + running track
Time keepers:	Jan, Jeff, Mike, Eve

Time keeper's tasks:

	8:30 AM – 9:30 AM:	marking out of the circuit
	10:00 AM – 12:30 PM:	each timekeeper keeps time for 2 participants. The times are noted on the score card and the best three times are passed to the co-workers
	12:30 PM:	removal of the equipment

Rules: 10 participants start every 20 minutes. Participants meet at the reception desk. The circuit consists of swimming (150 m), cycling (4 km), running (800 m).

Equipment: – 10 mountain bikes
                  – tracing ribbon
                  – 10 stopwatches
                  – 10 notebooks
                  – 10 pencils

Baseball

Manager:	John
Location:	soccer field
Referee:	John

Referee's tasks: 9:00 AM – 10:00 AM: placement of the equipment, make up the competition schedule
                    10:00 AM – 12:30 PM: lead the competition
                    13:30 PM – 16:30 PM: lead the competition
                    16:30 PM   removal of the equipment, pass the results on to the co-ordinator

Rules: Depending upon the number of teams, games are played in 2 or more groups. The following scores are given: 2 pts for winning, 1 pt for a draw and, if the game is lost, 0 pts. The winners of the subcompetition play for the final, the second for third and fourth place.

Equipment: – 2 baseball bats
                    – 20 tennis balls
                    – 10 bases

Basketball

Manager: Michael
Location: hall L4 for the girls
                    hall L5 for the boys
Referees: Michael, Wim
Scoreboard: some of the extra players
Co-workers' tasks: 9:00 AM – 10:00 AM: placement of the equipment, announcement of the competition timetable
                    10:00 AM – 12:30 PM: lead the competition
                    13:30 PM – 16:30 PM: lead the competition
                    16:30 PM: removal of the equipment, pass the results on to the co-ordinator.

Rules: The games are played following the usual regulations. Each match takes 2 x 12 minute halves (continuous game time), with a 5 minute break. "Time-outs" are not allowed. In case of a draw, the match is decided by 2 series of 3 free throws.

Equipment: – 5 basketballs
                    – 2 scoreboards
                    – 2 benches
                    – match papers
                    – a large piece of paper + marker pens

Table Tennis

Manager:	Frederick
Location:	hall L6
Teacher of initiation	
Courses:	Marc
Tasks:	8:30 AM – 10:00 AM: placement of the tables, announcement of the competition timetable
	10:00 AM – 12:30 PM: Marc gives initiation courses, Frederick leads the competitions
	13:30 PM – 16:30 PM: Marc gives initiation courses, Frederick leads the competitions
	16:30 PM: removal of the equipment, pass the results on to the co-ordinator.
Rules:	Each match follows the normal table tennis rules. The players count the scores themselves. At the end of the match, they pass the points on to the manager of the table tennis.
Equipment:	– 10 table tennis tables + nets
	– 20 table tennis paddles
	– 20 balls
	– a large piece of paper + marker pen

Mini Soccer

Manager:	Bart
Location:	soccer field
Referee:	Bart
Co-workers' tasks:	8:30 AM – 10:00 AM: placement of the equipment, announcement of the competition timetable
	10:00 AM – 12:30 PM: lead the competition
	13:30 PM – 16:30 PM: lead the competition
	16:30 PM: removal of the equipment, pass the results on to the co-ordinator.
Rules:	Each match takes half an hour and follows the normal rules of mini soccer. The winner of the match gets 2 pts, the looser receives 0 pts and, in case of a draw, each team gets 1 pt.
Equipment:	– 2 (mini) soccer goals
	– 10 soccer balls
	– large piece of paper + marker pen
	– ribbon

Open Swimming Event

Manager:	Jan
Location:	swimming pool
Co-workers:	Eve, Jeff, Monica

Co-workers' tasks:

12:30 PM – 13:30 PM:	placement of the equipment
13:30 PM – 13:40 PM:	hydrobics
13:40 PM – 14:10 PM:	lead the open swimming event
14:10 PM – 14:20 PM:	take pupils to the locker-rooms
14:20 PM – 14:30 PM:	hydrobics
14:30 PM – 15:00 PM:	lead the open swimming event
15:00 PM – 15:10 PM:	second group to the locker-rooms
15:10 PM – 15:20 PM:	hydrobics
15:20 PM – 15:50 PM:	lead the open swimming event
15:50 PM – 16:00 PM:	third group to the locker-rooms
16:00 PM:	removal of the equipment

Equipment:
- running mat
- 20 car tyres
- 6 sticking plates to be able to fix something to the floor
- 2 large floating mats
- 15 plastic balls
- diving equipment
- 4 hoops

(A practical example of an open swimming event can be found on pages 127 to 133)

Power Training & Fitness Training

Manager:	Sebastian
Location:	power room
Co-workers:	Sebastian, Hilde
Co-ordinators' tasks:	9:00 AM - 10:00 AM: check the equipment
	10:00 AM - 11:00 AM: light warm up + supervise pupils during a general session of fitness exercises (long series with light weights)
	11:00 AM - 12:00 PM: light warm up + supervise pupils during a general session of fitness exercises (long series with light weights)
	13:30 PM -14:30 PM: light warm up + supervise pupils during a general session of fitness exercises (long series with light weights)
	14:30 PM -15:30 PM: light warm up + supervise the pupils during power exercises (long series with heavier weights)
	15:30 PM -16:30:PM: light warm up + supervise the pupils during power exercises (long series with heavier weights)
Equipment:	– equipment present in the power room
	– dumb-bells from the sports service

Gymnastics

Manager:	Gary
Location:	hall L1
Co-workers:	Iris, Annick, Steven
Co-workers' tasks:	9:00 AM - 10:00 AM: placement of the equipment
	10:00 AM - 12:00 PM: lead the open gymnastics event
	13:30 PM - 16:30 PM: lead the open gymnastics event
	16:30 PM: removal of the equipment
Equipment:	– 4 horizontal bars
	– tumbling mats
	– 2 small trampolines, 1 double small trampoline
	– 10 thick mats, 20 small mats
	(A practical example of an open gymnastics event can be found on pages 176 to 180)

Aerobics/Step-aerobics

Manager:	George	
Location:	mirror room (judo room)	
Co-workers:	Sigrid	
Co-workers' tasks:	9:00 AM – 10:00 AM:	preparation/placement of the equipment
	10:30 AM – 11:00 AM:	teach aerobics
	11:30 AM – 12:00 PM:	teach step-aerobics
	14:00 PM – 14:30 PM:	teach aerobics
	15:00 PM – 15:30 PM:	teach step-aerobics
	16:00 PM – 16:30 PM:	teach aerobics
	16:30 PM:	removal of the equipment
Equipment:	– stereo	
	– 20 steps	

Eurofit-test

Manager:	John	
Location:	gallery	
Co-workers:	the Eurofit-team	
Co-workers' tasks:	8:30 AM – 10:00 AM:	placement of the equipment
	10:00 AM – 12:00 PM:	administer tests
	13:30 PM – 16:30 PM:	administer tests
	16:30 PM:	removal of the equipment
Equipment:	– the Eurofit-team brings the necessary equipment	

Mountain biking

Manager:	Sissy
Location:	forest
Co-workers:	Mina, Luc

Co-worker's tasks:

9:00 AM – 10:00 AM:	prepare and check the mountain bikes
10:00 AM – 11:00 AM:	lead the pupils through the bike circuit (10 pupils per group)
11:00 AM – 12:00 PM:	lead the pupils through the bike circuit (10 pupils per group)
13:30 PM – 14:30 PM:	lead the pupils through the bike circuit (10 pupils per group)
14:30 PM – 15:30 PM:	lead the pupils through the bike circuit (10 pupils per group)
15:30 PM – 16:30 PM:	lead the pupils through the bike circuit (10 pupils per group)

Note: 3 groups always leave at the same time

Walking Tour

Manager:	Christine
Location:	starting at the reception desk, the tour follows a circuit over the whole campus
Co-workers:	people from the reception desk

Co-workers' tasks:

10:00 AM – 12:00 PM:	give information about the tour and the envelope with the description of the route to the participants and collect it afterwards
13:30 PM – 16:00 PM:	give information about the tour and the envelope with the description of the route to the participants and collect it afterwards
16:00 PM:	the manager works out a final ranking order and gives the results to the co-ordinator

Organisation of the Meals

Manager:	Mina (cafeteria manager)
Location:	cafeteria

4) Evaluation Phase

4.1 General Remarks

– A generally positive evaluation from the participants and the co-ordinators.
– The objectives set forward were reached.
– Capacity participation by the right target group was reached during this event (496 pupils + 27 co-workers), the demand was even larger than the offer (174 pupils from 4 schools were not accepted to participate because there was not enough space).
– The sports and side activities generally went very well: the table tennis competition and the walking tour, however, had only a few participants.
– 4 groups were planned for the organisation of the meals. However the whole group arrived at the cafeteria at the same time. But the queue moved relatively quickly.
– The sign posting was not always very clear.
– On the external fields extra garbage bags should be provided.

4.2 Financial Evaluation

Expenses:	$ 2 x 496 pupils =	$ 992
Income:	printing costs	266
	copy card	120
	transport costs	192
	teachers' expenses	192
	purchase/rental of equipment	200
		$ 970

Therefore thanks to sponsoring almost all the expenses were covered and the event account closed with a small profit ($ 22).

4.3 Sponsorship

Equipment:	"Sportfresh":	(drinks)
	"Xantus":	(40 mountain bikes)
Prizes:	"Bintaxs"	
	"Aljolo"	

4.4 Conclusion

- The sports day was a success.
- The participants, as well as the co-workers, were happy with the programme.
- The physical education students responsible for the teaching learned a lot from this educational experience.

PART 2

RECREATIONAL CIRCUITS

1. Ball-games Circuit

1) Activities and Organisational Form

20 ball games are offered in a rotation system. The winner is the team with the most points (maximum = 200).

2) Location

Sports hall/playground.

3) Target group

- young people and adults
- teams have to be composed of 6 participants.

4) Practical Organisation

4.1 Leadership
- 1 co-ordinator
- 1 game leader per game = 20 game leaders.

4.2 Organisation
- Each game should be explained and if necessary demonstrated also
- Participants get about 1 minute to practise.
- The game leaders note the score and send the team on to the next game (the scoresheet has to be given to the team).
- Set up the order of the games in such a way that each time a different skill is used (for example: 1 = soccer, 2 = handball, 3 = basketball, etc).
- The game leaders have to make sure that all team participants can participate equally in the game.

Note:
- The maximum score for each game is 10.
- The secretary gives each team a scoresheet and a team name as well as a number indicating where the circuit should be started.
- Each game lasts 2 minutes: if the maximum score is achieved in less than 2 minutes the game stops.

4.3 Scoresheet

Team:
Starting number:

NUMBER	GAME	SCORE (.../10)
1	Hoop shooting	
2	Mini soccer	
3	Ball juggling	
4	Ball diving	
5	Hoop scoring	
6	Scoring in handball goal	
7	Hoop rolling	
8	Korfball goaling	
9	Lay-up	
10	Tour de France	
11	Wall ball	
12	Kangaroo ball	
13	Skipping relay	
14	Balance basketball	
15	Trampoline basketball	
16	Dribbling circuit	
17	Hoop ball	
18	Surprise ball	
19	Medicine ball throwing	
20	Ball passing	
	TOTAL	**/ 200**

4.4 Duration
Half a day.

5) Description of the games

5.1 Hoop shooting

Try to shoot the ball through the hoops from the 6 m-line. Each hoop is worth a specific number of points. Players shoot one after another. Everyone has 2 tries.

scoring: 185 – 200 = 10 pts
165 – 180 = 9 pts
145 – 160 = 8 pts
125 – 140 = 7 pts
105 – 120 = 6 pts
85 – 100 = 5 pts
65 – 80 = 4 pts
45 – 60 = 3 pts
25 – 40 = 2 pts
0 – 20 = 1 pt

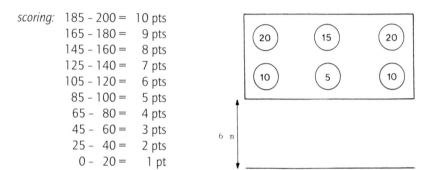

(handball goal, 6 hoops, rope, 6 soccer balls)

5.2 Mini soccer

The first player dribbles the ball around the cones to the second line where they try to shoot the ball to the box. Afterwards the player retrieves the ball, runs back and passes the ball to the next player.

scoring: 1 goal =   1 pt
10 goals = 10 pts

(2 box parts, 6 cones, 1 mini soccer ball)

Alternative in case of lack of room:
- The distance between the starting and the second line can be decreased by placing the cones further away from each other (i.e., wider apart).
- The parts of the box can also be placed lengthways and closer to the second line.

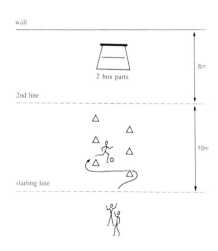

5.3 Ball juggling

Juggle with the ball for as long as possible, without interruption (soccer rules). The best performance (= number of contacts with the ball) for each of the players of the team is added up.

scoring:				
60 =	10 pts		35 =	5 pts
55 =	9 pts		30 =	4 pts
50 =	8 pts		25 =	3 pts
45 =	7 pts		20 =	2 pts
40 =	6 pts		15 =	1 pt

(1 soccer ball)

5.4 Ball diving

In turn, 2 players from the team throw the ball from behind the goal. The other players try to dive on to the mat and shoot the ball directly in the goal with their foot, head, etc. Then they retrieve the ball and give it to the shooter.

scoring:				
20 goals =	10 pts		10 goals =	5 pts
18 goals =	9 pts		8 goals =	4 pts
16 goals =	8 pts		6 goals =	3 pts
14 goals =	7 pts		4 goals =	2 pts
12 goals =	6 pts		2 goals =	1 pt

(2 mini soccer balls, 1 handball goal, mat)

5.5 Hoop scoring

Throw the handball from a distance of about 10 m through one of the hoops. Retrieve the ball.

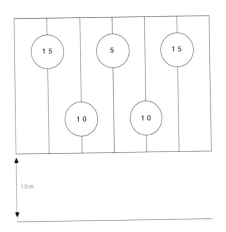

scoring:	
185 – 200 =	10 pts
165 – 180 =	9 pts
145 – 160 =	8 pts
125 – 140 =	7 pts
105 – 120 =	6 pts
85 – 100 =	5 pts
65 – 80 =	4 pts
45 – 60 =	3 pts

```
25 - 40 =    2 pts
 0 - 20 =    1 pt
```
(1 handball goal, 5 hoops, 6 handballs, rope)

5.6 Scoring in a handball goal

The players throw the ball in turn from the 6 m-line. The game leader is the goal-keeper.

scoring:			
20 goals =	10 pts	10 goals =	5 pts
18 goals =	9 pts	8 goals =	4 pts
16 goals =	8 pts	6 goals =	3 pts
14 goals =	7 pts	4 goals =	2 pts
12 goals =	6 pts	2 goals =	1 pt

(1 handball goal, 6 handballs)

5.7 Hoop rolling

2 players roll the hoop over a distance of about 10 m. The other players try to throw as many balls as possible through the hoop. Record the highest score.

scoring:	
10 balls =	10 pts
9 balls =	9 pts
8 balls =	8 pts
7 balls =	7 pts
6 balls =	6 pts
5 balls =	5 pts
4 balls =	4 pts
3 balls =	3 pts
2 balls =	2 pts
1 ball =	1 pt

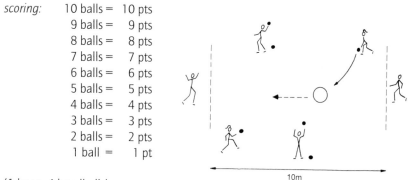

10m

(1 hoop, 4 handballs)

5.8 Korfball goaling

Try to throw as many balls as possible into the korfball hoop from outside the basketball circle in 2 minutes.

scoring:			
60 x =	10 pts	50 x =	8 pts
55 x =	9 pts	45 x =	7 pts

40 x =	6 pts	25 x =	3 pts
35 x =	5 pts	20 x =	2 pts
30 x =	4 pts	15 x =	1 pt

(1 korfball goal, 6 mini soccer balls)

5.9 Lay-up

Player 1 dribbles the ball to the basket, does a lay-up, dribbles back and passes the ball to the next player.

scoring:		
	6 goals =	10 pts
	5 goals =	9 pts
	4 goals =	8 pts
	3 goals =	6 pts
	2 goals =	4 pts
	1 goal =	2 pts

(1 basketball, 1 basketball hoop)

5.10 Tour de France

In turn, each of the players tries to shoot the ball into the basketball hoop from position 1; if they score, they can throw from position 2, etc. until they arrive at position 10 for a final throw.

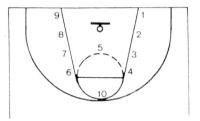

scoring: 2 goals = 1 pt

(1 basketball hoop, 6 basketballs)

5.11 Wall ball

The first player throws the ball against the wall. After the first bounce of the ball, the second player tries to bounce the ball back against the wall using a volleyball technique. The longest set counts as the final score.

scoring:				
	30 x =	10 pts	15 x =	5 pts
	27 x =	9 pts	12 x =	4 pts
	24 x =	8 pts	9 x =	3 pts
	21 x =	7 pts	6 x =	2 pts
	18 x =	6 pts	3 x =	1 pt

(1 volleyball)

5.12 Kangaroo ball

Player 1 bounces on a kangaroo ball between the cones. Player 1 leaves the kangaroo ball at the finish line then dribbles back to the starting point with a basketball. Player 2 dribbles the ball to the finish line and than bounces back with the kangaroo ball, etc.

starting line   6m   finish line

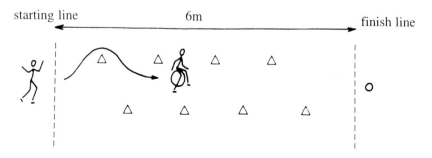

scoring: for each round (1x bouncing + 1x dribbling) = 1 pt

(1 kangaroo ball, 1 basketball, 8 cones)

5.13 Skipping relay
Player 1 skips with the volleyball between the legs, around cone 1, jumps over a rope and goes around cone 2. Then they carry the ball in the hands and run to the starting line, where they pass the ball on to the next player.

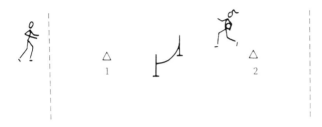

Note: if the player loses the ball, it must be retrieved and the player continues from the place where the ball was lost.

scoring: 6 x round = 10 pts   3 x round =   4 pts
             5 x round =   8 pts   2 x round =   2 pts
             4 x round =   6 pts

(1 volleyball, 2 cones, 2 posts/stands, rope)

5.14 Balance basketball
The players take a basketball and climb up the bench and along to the middle of the beam, try to score, jump down afterwards and retrieve the ball so they can start again.

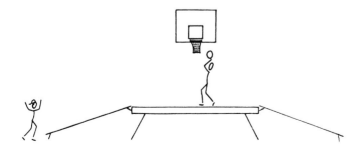

scoring:	20 goals =	10 pts	10 goals =	5 pts
	18 goals =	9 pts	8 goals =	4 pts
	16 goals =	8 pts	6 goals =	3 pts
	14 goals =	7 pts	4 goals =	2 pts
	12 goals =	6 pts	2 goals =	1 pt

(3 basketballs, 2 benches, balance beam, basketball hoop)

5.15 Trampoline basketball

Run along the bench, jump on the trampoline and on to the box. As the players jump off the box, they try to score. Catch the ball and run back (after the first attempt, the next player starts).

scoring: every goal is worth 1 pt

(1 bench, 1 mini trampoline, 1 box, 1 basketball hoop, 1 thick mat)

5.16 Dribbling circuit

While dribbling the ball, the player runs under the horizontal bar, jumps on to the box with the ball in hand, dribbles to the hoops, jumps with two feet into the hoops, dribbles between the cones and at the finish line tries to knock down a cone.

scoring: 1 round = 1 pt

(1 horizontal bar, 1 trampoline, 1 box, 1 thick mat, 4 hoops, 7 cones, 1 basketball)

5.17 Hoop ball
Throw the ball through the hoop, follow the ball, and get in line on the other side of the hoop. Continue the exercise from this side, etc.

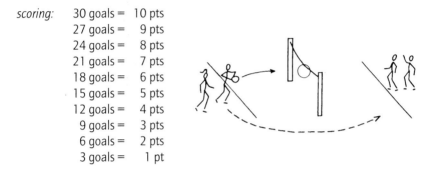

scoring:

30 goals =	10 pts
27 goals =	9 pts
24 goals =	8 pts
21 goals =	7 pts
18 goals =	6 pts
15 goals =	5 pts
12 goals =	4 pts
9 goals =	3 pts
6 goals =	2 pts
3 goals =	1 pt

(1 hoop, 2 posts/stands, rope, 1 handball)

5.18 Surprise ball
From behind the cone throw the ball over the thick mat to the other side where the ball is caught without letting it land on the ground. Run to the back of the line and continue the exercise.

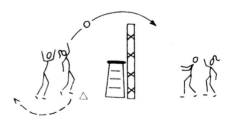

scoring: the longest set counts:
7 passes = 1 pt

(1 cone, 1 box, 1 thick mat, 1 handball)

5.19 Medicine ball throwing
A player sitting with legs spread wide apart throws the ball backwards. The next player throws again from the place where the ball lands on the floor.

scoring: 20 m = 1 pt, for each additional 3 m = 1 pt extra

(1 medicine ball, measuring tape)

5.20 Ball passing

The players lie on their backs one behind the other and pass the ball to one another with their feet. After making the pass, go to the end of the line.

scoring: Passing the ball from the first till the last = 2 pts
                          Maximum of 5 rounds = 10 pts

(1 volleyball)

6) Organisational scheme

hoop shooting	lay-up		hoop passing
	hoop ball	mini soccer	hoop scoring
ball diving			
trampoline basketball	kangaroo ball	surprise ball	ball juggling
			medicine ball throwing
			balance basketball
hoop rolling	scoring in a handball goal		korfball goaling
	Tour de France	skipping relay	dribbling circuit	wall ball

7) Equipment

- 1 medicine ball
- 16 hoops
- 9 mini soccer balls
- 7 soccer balls
- 4 handball goals
  (in case of lack of goals, they can be drawn on the wall)
- 25 cones
- 18 handballs
- 2 box parts + 3 boxes
- 1 mini goal
- 3 thick mats
- 23 volleyballs
- 1 korfball post/stand + basket
- 4 basketball hoops
- 12 basketballs
- 1 kangaroo ball
- 1 balance beam
- 3 benches
- 1 trampoline
- 1 horizontal bar
- 4 posts
- rope
- measuring tape
- numbers from 1-20
- scoresheets
- pencils
- metrestick

2. Soccer Circuit

1) Activities and organisational form

Soccer skills tests with a pass through system (the order is not defined).

2) Location

Soccer field.

3) Target group

- young people from 10-18
- soccer players.

4) Practical organisation

4.1 Leadership

- 1 co-ordinator
- 10 game leaders.

4.2 Organisation

- Each participant receives a scoresheet.
- The 10 tests must be accomplished by all participants (the order of the games is unrestricted).

- If all tests are completed you can ask for a second scoresheet.
- The player with the most points is the winner.

Note: Some tests can be doubled (or be taken from more than one player at the same time).

4.3 Scoresheet

NAME: _____

Game	Score
Target shooting	_____
Ball juggling	_____
Precision throw in	_____
Distance throw in	_____
Pass through the bridge	_____
Dribble with turn	_____
Ball control	_____
Long, high pass	_____
Header	_____
Obstacle course	_____
	TOTAL: _____

4.4 Duration
Half a day (depends on the number of participants).

5) Description of the games

5.1 Target shooting
The goal is divided into squares by means of ropes.
The player can kick 10 balls towards the goal from the goal area.

Note: When the ball touches a rope, the highest score is awarded.

(10 soccer balls, goal, rope)

10	8	10
8	4	8
6	2	6

10m

5.2 Ball juggling

Keep the ball in the air for as long as possible (soccer rules).
The highest number of contacts counts.

(1 soccer ball)

5.3 Precision throw in

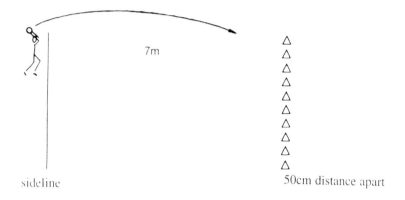

Throw the ball as precisely as possible from the sideline. 10 cones are placed 7 m from the sideline at 50 cm intervals. Each cone hit (with a correct throw in) is worth 10 pts. Each player can throw 10 times.

(1 soccer ball, 10 cones)

5.4 Distance throw in

The player has to try to throw the ball as far as possible into the field from the sideline (following soccer rules). Each player can throw 5 times. The distances are counted in meters.

(1 soccer ball, 1 metrestick)

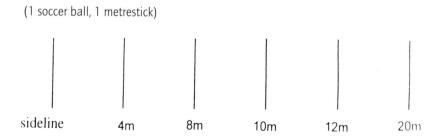

5.5 Pass through the bridge

5 balls are positioned behind a cone at a distance of 10 m from a "bridge" (0.5-1 m high). Kick the balls directly through the bridge (without touching it), and then do the same thing from the cone on the other side. Each ball which is kicked through the bridge is worth 10 pts.

Note: – The ball goes through the bridge: 10 pts.
– The ball goes through the bridge but touches it: 6 pts.
– The ball touches the bridge but does not go through it: 3 pts.

(2 cones, 2 posts/stands, rope, 5 soccer balls)

5.6 Dribble with turn

The player starts at the first cone, goes around it with the ball at the foot, dribbles to the second cone, does the same thing and again at the third. At the fourth cone, the player turns halfway around, runs as fast as possible to the first cone and starts again. Each correctly turned cone is worth 10 pts. The duration of the exercise is 1 minute. The maximum score is 100 pts. The distance between the cones is 4 m.

(4 cones, 1 soccer ball)

start line

5.7 Ball control

The player kicks the ball from the hands upwards (at least 3 m) and controls it in one time with the inside or outside foot.

This exercise has to be done 10 times. Each correct control (according to the gameleader) is worth 10 pts.

(1 soccer ball)

5.8 Long, high pass

Behind the first cone, there are 10 balls. Dribble to the second cone, which is 20 m away, and from there shoot in an arc into one of the 4 hoops (which lie on the ground). Points are awarded when the ball falls in one of the hoops.

Note: For "left-footed" players you have to change the direction (and the scoring).

(4 hoops, 10 soccer balls, 2 pins)

5.9 Header

Try to head a ball (which you kick from the ground with your foot) directly into the goal. 5 bike tyres hang at different heights (25 cm, 50 cm, 75 cm, 100 cm, 125 cm under the cross bar). You should try to head the ball through one of the tyres from a distance of 4 m. Each successful attempt is worth 1 pt.

(5 bike tyres, 1 goal, 1 soccer ball)

5.10 Obstacle circuit

The player has to cover the distance as fast as possible and do all the tasks correctly.

Task 1: dribble the ball with your feet between the cones (distance 1 m).
Task 2: pass the ball under the hurdles (0.50-1 m) and jump over the hurdles. The distance between two hurdles is 2 m delete.
Task 3: head the ball from one cone to another (distance = 3 m).
Task 4: juggle the ball from one cone to another (distance = 7 m).
Task 5: kick the ball from the hands with a volley into box 1: there it can bounce once, afterwards you have to play it directly (or by juggling) in box 2 ... (5 x = 5 boxes of 2 m).

(12 cones, 1 soccer ball, 4 hurdles, stopwatch, 5 boxes marked on the grounds)

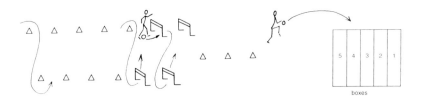

6) Organisational scheme

long, high pass				
distance throw in				
precision throw in	ball control	dribble with turn	obstacle circuit	
pass through the bridge				
target shooting	ball juggling	header		

7) Equipment

- scoresheet
- pencils
- task boards
- rope
- 30 balls
- chalk
- stopwatch

- 4 hurdles or gates (0.50-1 m)
- 5 bike tyres
- 4 hoops
- 2 poles + rope (gate)
- 1 metrestick
- 2 goals

Note: You have to adapt the balls to the age of the players, or you can use different kinds of balls.

3. Basketball Circuit

1) Activities and organisational form

Basketball skills tests in a rotating system
(free order).

2) Location

Sports hall.

3) Target group

- young people from 10-18
- basketball players.

4) Practical organisation

4.1 Leadership
- 1 general coordinator
- 10 game leaders.

4.2 Organisation
- Each competitor gets a scoresheet.
- All tests must be completed. The order of the games is unrestricted.
- If all tests are done, you can get a second scoresheet.
- The player with the highest number of points is the winner.

Note: Some tests can be repeated or be done by groups of 2 players.

4.3 Scoresheet

NAME: _____

Game	Score
Shot on goal	
Bullet pass	
Overhead pass	
Chest pass	
Corner shot	
Dribbling speed	
Free throw	
Under the basket	
Lay up	
Shoot right where you are	

TOTAL: _____

4.4 Duration
About 30 minutes per scoresheet (depends on the number of participants).

5) Description of the games

5.1 Shot on goal

From each of the 2 marked places (see figure) shoot the ball into the basket 10 times. Any way of throwing the ball with one or both hands is permitted. You get 2 pts for each basket, 1 pt if it just touches the ring.

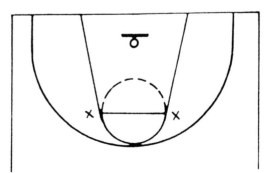

(1 basket, 1 basketball, chalk)

5.2 Bullet pass

The player stands 3 m from the wall and throws the ball against it at head height. Catch the ball (directly or with a bounce) and throw it back against the wall. Repeat 20 times as fast as possible. Any method is permitted, as long as you really catch the ball and throw it back and not just hit it back. If the ball falls, you have to recover it and carry on from behind the line. You get 2 tries. The score is based on the quickest time to do 20 passes.

scoring:

35 secs or less = 40 pts	44 – 45 secs =	15 pts
36 – 37 secs = 35 pts	46 – 47 secs =	10 pts
38 – 39 secs = 30 pts	48 – 49 secs =	5 pts
40 – 41 secs = 25 pts	50 secs or more =	1 pt
42 – 43 secs = 20 pts		

(1 basketball, 1 stopwatch, chalk)

5.3 Overhead pass (precision)

The player stands 8 m from a wall with a target on it (set 1 m from the ground) and throws the ball with one hand overhead to the target. Each player gets 20 tries. During the throw one step is allowed, but both feet have to remain behind the line.

scoring: 3 pts for a throw in the bull's-eye (diameter 50 cm)
2 pts for a throw in the inner ring (diameter 100 cm)
1 pt for a throw in the outer ring (diameter 150 cm)

(1 basketball, chalk)

5.4 Chest pass (precision)

The player stands 6 m from the wall and makes a two-handed pass towards the target (see 5.3 Overhead pass). Each player gets 20 tries.

Note: Adapt the height of the target to the age of the players.

(1 basketball, chalk)

5.5 Corner shot

The player stands 6 m from the basket in the corner of the court (sideways to the backboard). Each player attempts 10 throws from the left, 10 from the right. Single as well as two-handed throws are allowed. The game leader throws the ball back.

scoring:
2 pts for each basket
1 pt for just tou-
ching the ring

(1 basket, 1 basketball)

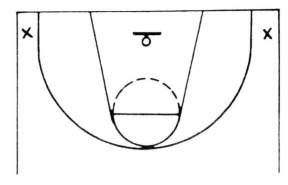

5.6 Dribbling speed

Dribble the ball as fast as possible around the cones and back. The best of 2 tries counts.

scoring:			
10 secs or less =	40 pts	19 – 20 secs =	15 pts
11 – 12 secs =	35 pts	21 – 22 secs =	10 pts
13 – 14 secs =	30 pts	23 – 24 secs =	5 pts
15 – 16 secs =	25 pts	25 secs or more =	1 pt
17 – 18 secs =	20 pts		

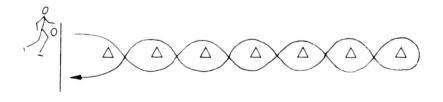

(7 cones, 1 basketball, 1 stopwatch)

5.7 Free throw

Any type of throw from the foul line is allowed.
20 tries, 2 pts per basket.

(1 basket, 1 basketball)

5.8 Under the basket

The player stands under the basket with a ball in hand.
Within 30 seconds try to score as many points as possible in any way. Pick-up the rebounds yourself.
2 attempts, 2 pts per basket.

(1 basket, 1 basketball, 1 stopwatch)

5.9 Lay-up

The player starts from the foul line, dribbles the ball towards the basket and does a lay-up, picks up the rebound and goes back to the foul line.
20 tries, 2 pts per basket.

(1 basket, 1 basketball)

5.10 Shoot-right-where-you-are

The player starts from the foul line, shoots the ball into the basket and picks up the rebound. Wherever the ball is caught, it can be thrown again.
20 tries, 2 pts per basket. If the ball goes off the court, the player starts 1 m inside the line where the ball went out.

(1 basket, 1 basketball)

6) Organisational scheme

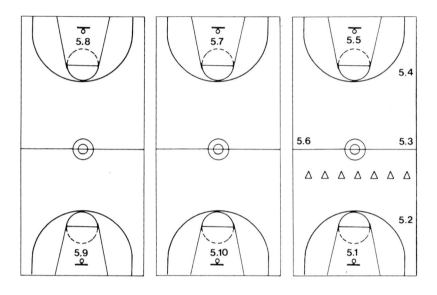

7) Equipment

-     10 basketballs
-     6 baskets
-     6 cones
-     3 stopwatches
-     chalk

4. Volleyball Circuit

1) Activities and organisational form

Volleyball skills tests in no fixed order.

2) Location

Volleyball court.

3) Target group

– young people from 10-18
– volleyball players.

4) Practical organisation

4.1 Leadership
– 1 general co-ordinator
– 10 game leaders.

4.2 Organisation
– Each competitor gets a scoresheet.
– All tests must be completed. The order of the games is unrestricted.
– When all the tests are done, you can get a second scoresheet.
– The player with the highest number of points is the winner.

Note: Some tests can be repeated or can be done by groups.4.3

4.3 Scoresheet

NAME: _____

Game	Score
Precision serve	_____
Sets	_____
Digging	_____
Set to a target	_____
Juggling	_____
Distance set	_____
Obstacle shooting	_____
Set into a goal	_____
Precision set	_____
Spike	_____
	TOTAL: _____

4.4 Duration
About 30 minutes per scoresheet (depends on the number of participants).

5) Description of the games

5.1 Precision serve
Try to serve the ball from the serving line and aim at a certain spot (e.g., a mat).
Each player gets 10 attempts.

scoring: on the line = 1 pt   in the square = 2 pts

(1 volleyball, 1 volleyball net, 1 mat)

5.2 Sets
From 5 m set towards a square (30 x 30 cm) marked on the wall.
Each player gets 20 sets.

scoring: 1 goal = 1 pt   20 goals = 20 pts

(1 volleyball, chalk)

5.3 Digging

From 5 m dig the ball towards a square (30 x 30 cm) marked on the wall. Each player gets 20 sets.

scoring: 1 goal = 1 pt   20 goals = 20 pts

(1 volleyball, chalk)

5.4 Set to a target

A target has been drawn on a mat placed behind the 3 m line. Set the ball over the net into the target. A bull's-eye is 2 pts, the centre circle is 1 pt. Each player has 20 attempts.

scoring:			
30 = 20 pts		19 - 20 = 10 pts
29 = 19 pts		17 - 18 = 9 pts
28 = 18 pts		15 - 16 = 8 pts
27 = 17 pts		13 - 14 = 7 pts
26 = 16 pts		11 - 12 = 6 pts
25 = 15 pts		9 - 10 = 5 pts
24 = 14 pts		7 - 8 = 4 pts
23 = 13 pts		5 - 6 = 3 pts
22 = 12 pts		3 - 4 = 2 pts
21 = 11 pts		1 - 2 = 1 pt

(1 volleyball, 1 mat)

5.5 Juggling

While sitting down, throw the ball upwards, quickly stand up and catch the ball without dropping it.
Each player gets 5 attempts. The highest score counts.

scoring: 1 x sit and stand up = 1 pt   20 x and more = 20 pts

(1 volleyball)

5.6 Distance set

Set the ball as far as possible
Each player has 10 attempts. The highest score counts.

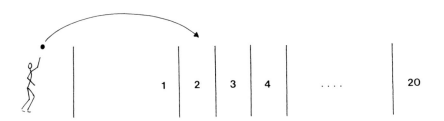

scoring: 20 = 20 pts
1 = 1 pt

(1 volleyball)

5.7 Obstacle shooting

Setting and/or digging the volleyball, take a table tennis ball out of a bucket, keep the ball bouncing while walking to a second bucket, into which you drop the ball. If the ball falls, you lose it. Each player gets 10 table tennis balls. From the moment the player stops shooting (holds the ball in the hands or lets the ball fall), the game finishes.

scoring: 1 ball into the bucket = 2 pts   20 balls into the bucket = 20 pts

(10 table tennis balls, 1 volleyball, 2 buckets)

5.8 Set into a goal

Set the ball through a hoop into a goal.
Each player gets 10 attempts.

scoring: touching the hoop = 1 pt   through the hoop = 2 pts

(1 handball goal,
1 volleyball, 1 hoop,
2 ropes)

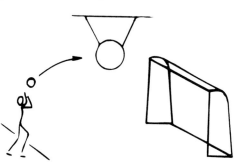

5.9 Precision set

The game leader (x) gives sets to the player (o); the player hits or sets the ball over the net towards one of the 2 hoops which are in the field.
Each player gets 10 attempts.

scoring: touching the hoop = 1 pt   into the hoop= 2 pts

net

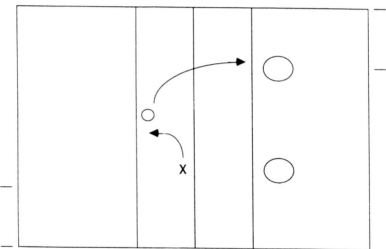

(2 hoops, 1 volleyball, 1 volleyball net)

5.10 Spike

From a cone (3 m from the wall) spike the balls using the floor against the wall and spike the rebounding ball immediately. The player tries to make the longest series possible.
Each player gets 5 attempts. The longest series counts.

scoring: 1 = 1 pt   20 and more = 20 pts

(1 volleyball, 1 cone)

6) Organisational scheme

Note: If there is only one volleyball field, games 5.4 and 5.9 can be played over a rope.

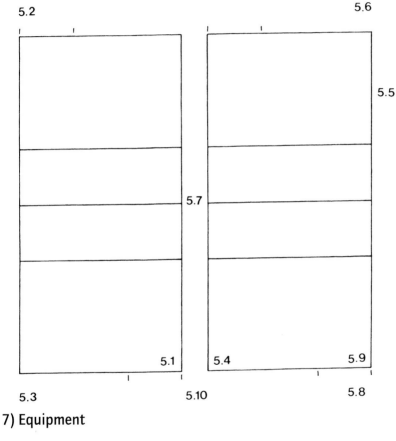

7) Equipment

- scoresheets
- pencils
- message boards
- 1 cone
- chalk
- rope
- 1 stopwatch
- 10 volleyballs

- 2 mats
- 10 table tennis balls
- 2 buckets
- 4 hoops
- 1 handball goal
- 2 volleyball nets
- 4 volleyball poles

5. Handball Circuit

1) Activities and organisational form

Tests of handball skills with a rotating system.

2) Location

Sports hall.

3) Target group

– young people from 10-18
– handball players.

4) Practical organisation

4.1 Leadership
– 1 general co-ordinator
– 10 game leaders.

4.2 Organisation
– 1 scoresheet per 2 players.
– All of the 10 tests must be done in the order indicated on the scoresheet.
– If all tests are done, you get a second sheet.
– The duo with the most points is the winner.

4.3 Scoresheet

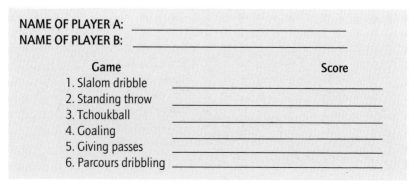

NAME OF PLAYER A:	
NAME OF PLAYER B:	
Game	**Score**
1. Slalom dribble	
2. Standing throw	
3. Tchoukball	
4. Goaling	
5. Giving passes	
6. Parcours dribbling	

7. Throwing at cones _____
8. Rolling target _____
9. Reversed goal _____
10. Distance throwing _____

TOTAL: _____/200

4.4 Duration
About 30 minutes per scoresheet (depends on the number of participants).

5) Description of the games

5.1 Slalom dribble
Player A starts at line 1, dribbles the ball in slalom around the cones to line 2, shoots at the mini goal, recovers the ball and dribbles it back in a straight line towards line 1. From there player B does the same. Each player gets 5 attempts. If the player loses the ball while dribbling, they should recover the ball and shoot from there.

scoring: 10 goals = 20 pts   1 goal = 1 pt

(1 mini goal, 5 cones, 1 handball)

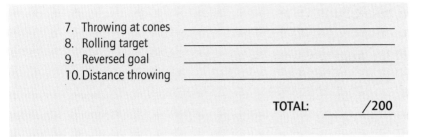

5.2 Standing throw
The players stand 6 m from the goal. Hoops hang in the goal, each hoop is worth a certain number of points. Each player has 10 attempts to score using a standing throw.
The points of both players are added together.

scoring: 58 – 60 = 20 pts
55 – 57 = 19 pts
52 – 54 = 18 pts
49 – 51 = 17 pts
46 – 48 = 16 pts
43 – 45 = 14 pts
40 – 42 = 13 pts
37 – 39 = 12 pts
34 – 36 = 11 pts
31 – 33 = 10 pts
28 – 30 = 9 pts
25 – 27 = 8 pts
22 – 24 = 7 pts
19 – 21 = 6 pts
16 – 18 = 5 pts
13 – 15 = 4 pts
10 – 12 = 3 pts
4 – 9 = 2 pts
1 – 3 = 1 pt

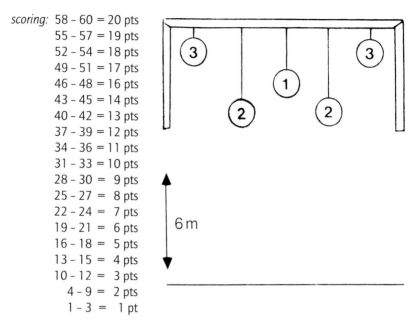

(5 hoops, rope, handball, handball goal)

5.3 Tchoukball

Both players stand 6 m from the tchouk or a small trampoline (placed at an angle). Player A throws the ball at the trampoline, player B catches the bouncing ball from behind the line and throws again at the trampoline. Both players try to make the longest series possible. They get 3 attempts. The longest series counts.

scoring: series of more than 20 = 20 pts   series of 20 = 19 pts

...

series of 3 = 2 pts   series of 2 = 1 pt

(1 tchouk or small trampoline, 1 handball)

5.4 Goaling

Both players try to score a goal from behind the 6 m-line. The game leader is the goal keeper. Each player has 16 attempts.

scoring: 20 goals = 20 pts   1 goal = 1 pt

(1 handball goal, 2 handballs)

5.5 Giving passes

Both players start from behind the mid-line and they run towards the goal while passing the ball to each other. The player who has the ball at the 6 m-line shoots. The game leader is the goalkeeper. The other player retrieves the ball and both players start again. They have 10 attempts. If the ball touches the ground, that attempt is over.

scoring: 20 goals = 20 pts   1 goal = 1 pt

(1 handball, 1 handball goal)

5.6 Parcours dribbling

Player A starts at the starting line, dribbles the ball towards the bench, runs across it while dribbling the ball next to it, then dribbles the ball towards the gate. While dribbling the ball, she/he crouches under the gate, dribbles on one leg to the cone, dribbles around it and comes back dribbling the ball, alternating hands each time. From there player B does the same. If the ball is lost, start again where the ball was lost. The time for both players is added together. Each player gets 2 attempts.

scoring: At the end all the times of the duos are put into order.
                   Fastest lap = 20 pts   Slowest lap = 10 pts

(1 handball, 1 cone, 1 bench, 1 gate)

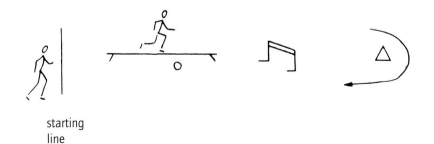

starting
line

5.7 Throwing at cones

6 cones are placed on a bench. Players stand 6 m from the cones. Each player gets 10 attempts to knock as many cones off the bench as possible. When all the cones have been knocked off, they should be replaced.

scoring: 20 cones or more = 20 pts   1 cone = 1 pt

(6 cones, 1 bench, 2 handballs)

5.8 Rolling target

Player A stands behind a line, player B stands 4 m away and rolls a hoop parallel with this line. Player A throws the ball through the rolling hoop. The ball must not touch the ground first. Each player gets 10 attempts.

scoring: 20 balls through the hoop = 20 pts   1 ball through the hoop = 1 pt

(1 hoop, 1 handball)

5.9 Reversed goal

A goal stands 2 m from the wall, with the opening towards the wall. Both players stand 6 m from the reversed goal. Each player gets 10 attempts to get the ball into the goal. The ball must bounce off the wall first. A ball which rolls into the goal does not count.

scoring: 20 goals = 20 pts   1 goal = 1 pt

(1 handball goal, 2 handballs)

5.10 Distance throwing

Each player starts at position 1 (3 m from the wall) and throws from there towards a 50 x 50 cm square marked on the wall, 1.5 m from the ground. If successful, move back to position 2 (about 1 m further away) and so on, until position 10 is reached. Each player gets 3 attempts.

scoring:
furthest   goal   (from number 10) = 10 pts closest goal (from number 1) = 1 pt Both players' scores are added together.

(1 handball, chalk, measuring tape)

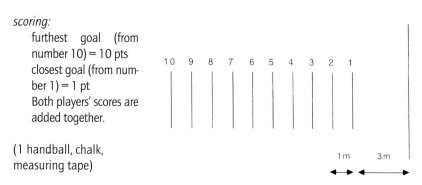

6) Organisational scheme

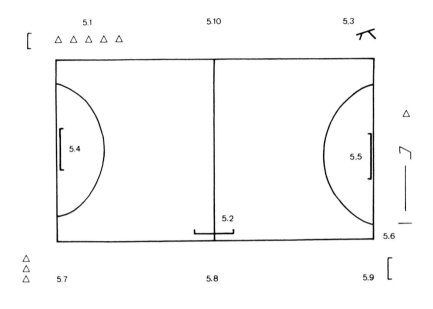

7) Equipment

- 6 hoops
- 2 benches
- 13 handballs
- 5 handball goals
- 1 small trampoline
- 13 cones

- rope
- chalk
- 1 gate (hurdle)
- 1 stopwatch
- 1 measuring tape
- 1 mini goal

6. Korfball Circuit

1) Activities and organisational form

Korfball skills tests with a rotating system.

2) Location

Sports hall.

3) Target group

- young people from 10-18
- korfball players.

4) Practical organisation

4.1 Leadership
- 1 co-ordinator
- 10 game leaders.

4.2 Organisation
- 1 scoresheet per 4 players.
- In each group of 4, 2 teams are created (A + B and C + D).
- The points for A + B are added together separately from the points for C + D.
- All of the 10 tests must be done in the order indicated on the scoresheet.
- The duo with the most points is the winner.
- If all of the 10 tests have been completed, each player can start again with another partner.

4.3 Scoresheet

NAME A: _____	NAME C: _____
NAME B: _____	NAME D: _____
Game	**Score**	**Score**
Throwing into a circle	_____	_____
Throwing into a target	_____	_____
Throwing into a goal	_____	_____

Fast throwing	_____	_____
Scoring 1	_____	_____
Running target	_____	_____
Mini korfball	_____	_____
Horse and rider	_____	_____
Scoring 2	_____	_____
Skills run	_____	_____
TOTAL:	_____	_____

4.4 Duration

About 40 minutes per scoresheet (depends on the number of participants).

5) Description of the games

5.1 Throwing into a circle

The players throw the ball over a rope, towards a circle drawn on the wall. If the ball hits the circle, it is worth 1 pt. Each player gets two series of 5 throws. The player with the highest score gets 4 pts, the one with the lowest 1 pt.

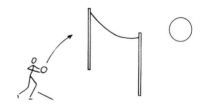

(2 poles, 1 rope, 1 ball, chalk)

5.2 Throwing into a target

A target is drawn on the wall. The player throws the ball from 5 m away with a chest pass towards the target. If the ball hits the target, the player gets 1 pt. Each player gets two series of 5 throws.
The player with the highest score gets 4 pts, the one with the lowest 1 pt.

(1 ball, chalk)

5.3 Throwing into a goal

From 5 m the player throws towards the korf. If the ball touches the korf, it is worth 1 pt. If it goes in, it is worth 2 pts. Each player gets 10 throws.

The player with the highest score gets 4 pts, the one with the lowest 1 pt.

(1 ball, 1 korfball pole + korf)

5.4 Fast throwing

From a distance of 3 m a player has to make as many chest passes against the wall as possible in 15 seconds. Each player gets 2 attempts.
The player with the highest score gets 4 pts, the one with the lowest 1 pt.

(1 ball, 1 stopwatch)

5.5 Scoring 1

Each player tries to score as many times as possible from any place in 1 minute. The throw has to be two-handed. Each goal is 1 pt.
The player with the highest score gets 4 pts, the one with the lowest 1 pt.

(1 ball, 1 korfball pole + korf, 1 stopwatch)

5.6 Running target

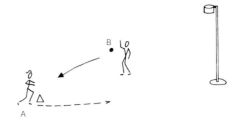

Player A starts at a cone, runs towards the korf, receives a pass from player B and shoots. Each goal is worth 2 pts. You get 1 pt if the ball touches the korf. Each player gets 10 attempts. Afterwards, players C and D do the same. The player with the highest score gets 4 pts, the one with the lowest 1 pt.

(2 cones, 1 ball, 1 korfball pole + korf)

5.7 Mini korfball

Players A + B start from the free throw line and each tries to score. If they succeed, the ball goes to players C + D who do the same. If the other team can intercept the ball before the players attempt to shoot, they win the ball and have to go to the free throw line before they can try to score. The team which makes 2 goals first, wins. The team with the 2 goals gets 4 pts. If the other team scored only 1 goal, they get 2 pts, otherwise they get 1 pt.

(1 ball, 1 korfball pole + korf, 1 field ribbon)

5.8 Horse and rider

Team 1 (players A + B) starts from the line. Player A takes the ball and jumps on the back of player B (horse and rider). Player B runs towards the cone and from there player A tries to score.

If the ball touches the korf, 1 pt is scored, scoring a korf is worth 2 pts. Player B retrieves the ball and runs back towards the finish line. Now player B jumps on the back of player A. Each player gets 3 balls. Team 2 (players C + D) does the same. The player with the highest score gets 4 pts, the one with the lowest score gets 1 pt.

(1 ball, 1 korfball pole + korf, 1 cone)

5.9 Scoring 2

Each team gets a ball. Both teams stand around the korf. Each team has to score a goal as fast as possible. The team that finishes first (making 10 goals), gets 4 pts. If the other team has more than 5 goals, they get 2 pts. If they have 5 or less, they get 1 pt.

(2 balls, 1 korfball pole + korf)

5.10 Skills run

Each player tries to cover the course as fast as possible without a ball by running around the cones from a towards b, sideways from b towards c, backwards from c towards d and also backwards from d towards e. Each player gets 2 attempts. The fastest lap counts. The player with the fastest lap gets 4 pts, the slowest 1 pt.

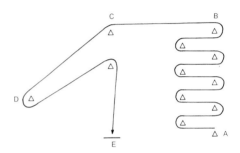

(12 cones, 1 stopwatch)

6) Organisational scheme

5.1	5.2	5.3	5.4
5.5	5.6	5.7	
5.8	5.9	5.10	

7) Equipment

- 10 balls
- 6 korfball poles + korf
- rope
- 2 poles

- 2 stopwatches
- chalk
- 15 cones
- 1 ribbon

7. Tennis Circuit

1) Activities and organisational form

Tests of tennis skills with a rotating system.

2) Location

Sports hall.

3) Target group

- young people from 12-18
- tennis players
- the circuit is designed for a maximum of 48 players.

4) Practical organisation

4.1 Leadership
- 1 general co-ordinator
- 6 game leaders (1 game leader for 3 to 4 games).

4.2 Organisation
- Groups of 2 players.
- All the games are numbered.
- Each group gets a different number. When you change, each group number increases by 1 (24 goes back to 1).
- Each game lasts 3 minutes. You get 1 minute to change games.
- Change at the whistle signal.
- There are no winners or losers. Just try to play the games as well as possible.

4.3 Duration
About 1 1/2 hours.

5) Description of the games

5.1 Back-hand
Player A throws a tennis ball to player B. Player B returns with a backhand.

(1 tennis ball, 1 racket)

5.2 Wall rally
Both players stand 2 m from the wall and try to make the longest rally. The ball has to bounce once before it is returned. The players hit the ball back in turn.

(1 tennis ball, 2 rackets)

5.3 Target tennis
Players try to hit a target which is drawn on the wall. The ball can bounce once and the players have to hit the ball alternately.

(1 tennis ball, 2 rackets)

5.4 Basket tennis
Both players stand at the side of a basket and try to hit the ball into the basket with a forehand.

(1 tennis ball, 2 rackets, 1 basket)

5.5 Wall volley
Player A tries to make the longest rally against the wall without letting the ball bounce. If the ball bounces on the floor, it is player B's turn.

(1 tennis ball, 2 rackets)

5.6 Amorti
Player A hits the ball towards player B, who tries to stop the ball on his or her racket (amorti). Then vice versa.

(1 tennis ball, 2 rackets)

5.7 Ball lifting

Both players try to find as many ways as possible to lift a ball without using their hands. After trying it out, both players try to lift the ball 10 times as fast as possible.

(1 tennis ball, 2 rackets)

5.8 Bouncing

Alternately bounce the ball 5 times on the ground and 5 times in the air. Then pass the ball to the other player. Try to make the longest rally.

(1 bench, 1 tennis ball, 2 rackets)

5.9 Swedish bench

Player A walks in a certain manner on the bench while bouncing the ball in the air. Player B has to copy it and vice versa.
Examples:
- walking forwards
- walking backwards

- with legs spread
- etc.

(2 tennis balls, 2 rackets)

5.10 Corner tennis

The same as wall tennis (wall rally or volley), but in a corner of the room.

(1 tennis ball, 2 rackets)

5.11 Rope tennis

A rope is hung 2 m high. From behind a line hit the ball over the rope, run behind the other line and hit it back. Try to do the longest series.

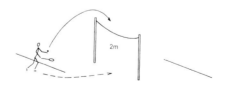

(1 tennis ball, 1 racket, 2 poles, rope)

5.12 Ball against the wall

Mark a line on the wall 1 m high from the ground. Each player hits the ball in turn. Try to make the longest series.

(1 tennis ball, 2 rackets)

5.13 Hoop tennis

Players are facing each other with a hoop in front of each of them. Each player aims for the other's hoop. The ball can bounce once.

(1 tennis ball, 2 rackets, 2 hoops)

5.14 Volley-volley in a hoop

Both players volley the ball to each other without leaving the hoop they are standing in.

(1 tennis ball, 2 rackets, 2 hoops)

5.15 Moving volley-volley

Players stand at a cone. They volley the ball to each other while moving towards the other cone.

(1 tennis ball, 2 rackets, 2 pins)

5.16 Hand tennis

The players hit the ball to each other with their hands.

(1 tennis ball)

5.17 Forehand over the net

The players hit the ball to each other with a forehand stroke over the net. The ball can bounce once.

(1 tennis ball, 2 rackets, 1 net)

5.18 Backhand over the net

The players hit the ball with a backhand over the net. The ball can bounce once.

(1 tennis ball, 2 rackets, 1 net)

5.19 Volley over the net

The players volley the ball over the net. The ball can bounce once.

(1 tennis ball, 2 rackets, 1 net)

5.20 Mini tennis with control bounce

Before returning the ball, the players have to control the ball by making it bounce an extra time on their racket.

(1 tennis ball, 2 rackets, 1 net)

5.21 Cone Slalom

Player A slaloms around the cones and returns to the starting line while bouncing the ball high all the time. Afterwards the ball is given to player B.

(1 tennis ball, 2 rackets, 6 cones)

5.22 Forehand

Player A throws the ball towards B, who returns it with a forehand stroke.

(1 tennis ball, 2 rackets)

5.23 Throw stop

Player A throws the ball towards B. Player B controls the ball with the racket.

(1 tennis ball, 2 rackets)

5.24 Throwing in a hoop

The players throw the ball to each other through a hoop placed on the floor. The ball bounces once.

(1 tennis ball, 1 hoop)

6) Organisational scheme

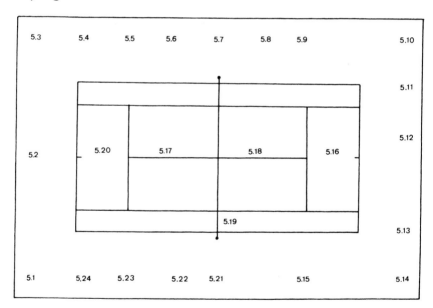

7) Equipment

- 5 hoops
- 26 tennis balls
- 1 racket per person
- 9 cones
- 1 basket
- 1 stopwatch

- elastic
- 1 rope + 2 poles
- 1 Swedish bench
- 24 signs
- nets

8. Swimming Circuit

1) Activities and organisational form

Circuits with different swimming skills exercises, through a rotating system.

2) Location

Swimming pool.

3) Target group

- mainly children, but it is also possible for adults
- swimmers of medium or higher level
- this example is for a group of about 50 participants.

4) Practical organisation

4.1 Leadership

- 1 co-ordinator
- 5 game leaders (1 per task).

4.2 Organisation

- The participants are divided into 5 groups (maximum of 10 participants per group), 1 group per circuit. You always start with 2 participants, and when those 2 arrive at the next task within the circuit, the next 2 are allowed to start.

- If everybody in the group has finished, the group could do the circuit for a second time.
- The skills in the circuit must be performed as well as possible, but speed is not important.
- 10 minutes is allowed for each task, then music is played and the teams move on.
- The game leader explains the game and shows the participants where to go for the next game.
- The game leaders set up the game with the first group they lead; the last group helps to put the equipment away.
- Each game leader writes a description and draws a sketch on a large piece of paper for his or her own game.

4.3 Duration
About 2 hours.

5) Description of the games

5.1 Surprise circuit
a) Fall backwards in the water with outstretched legs and holding the ankles with both hands.
b) "The St. Nicholas' bag": Place a plastic bag filled with objects underwater. Each participant handles the objects underwater and names as many objects as possible.
c) With a tennis ball in each fist, swim the crawl stroke without losing either ball. At the end you throw the tennis balls into a bucket.
d) Come back "waltzing" (one stroke of backstroke followed by one stroke of crawl, etc) to the middle of the pool.
e) For the second half invent a new swimming stroke.

(plastic bag with objects, 10 tennis balls, 1 bucket)

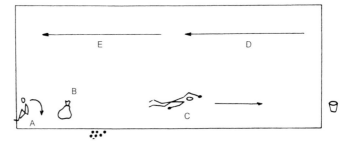

5.2 Disguise circuit

a) Put on a piece of clothing and swim across the pool. Peg the garment on a clothes line and swim back. When you have brought over 4 garments, put all of them back on and swim back to the starting line.
b) Here you exchange one piece of clothing with a partner.
c) Put all the garments in the water, wring them out above the water and transport them over 2 lengths of the pool.

(garments, clothes-line, clothes-pegs).

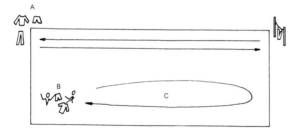

5.3 Obstacle circuit

a) Secure a floating mat in the pool: first crawl over it, then roll over it and then stand up.
b) Dive through 2 hoops.
c) Swim around the buoy.
d) Sit on a kick board and "drive the car" (move by alternating internal and external hand movements = sculling).
e) Crawl over a car tyre, crawl in the tyre and swim back to the other side.

(floating mat, 2 hoops, 2 kick boards, 2 bags of sand, 1 buoy, elastic line, 2 car tyres, 2 fixing plates)

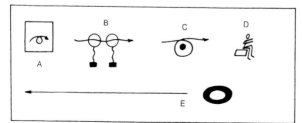

5.4 Underwater circuit

a)   Dive in and float as far as possible, (head) underwater.
b)   Swim underwater between 4 ribbons.

c) Gather 3 objects, one after the other (without surfacing). Bring the objects to the surface and swim back to the starting line.

d) By 2's: sing under water; the partner must guess the song.
e) By 2's: hold up a number of fingers; the partner must guess how many.
f) By exhaling sit or lie as flat as possible on the bottom of the pool.

(4 ribbons, 3 sinking objects)

5.5 Ball circuit

a) Crawl with a ball to the other side of the pool.
b) Throw the ball into a goal.
c) Come out of the water and dribble 10 times on the spot.
d) In shallow water, press the ball down with the legs, let it go and catch the ball without touching the water.
e) Try to swim with the ball to the bottom of the pool.
f) By 2's: throw the ball to each other, 10 times with 2 hands, 10 times with 1 hand.

(beach balls, water polo goal)

6) Organisational scheme

5.5	5.3	5.4	5.2	5.1

7) Equipment

- 2 hoops
- running mat
- buoy
- 2 car tyres
- 2 kick boards
- 2 fixing plates
- elastic line
- 4 ribbons
  (with weights down below to anchor them)

- 10 tennis balls
- 1 bucket
- garments
- clothes-pegs + clothes-line
- plastic bag with objects
- 2 sinking objects
- 1 water polo goal

PART 3

RECREATIONAL TOURNAMENTS

9. Open Tournament

1) Activities and organisational form

A whole range of stroke games, offered on a "come and go" basis, combined with a challenge system (ladder tournament).

2) Location

Sports hall or playground (protected from the wind).

3) Target group

Because of the varied offer of activities very heterogeneous groups (children, young people, adults) can participate. In this type of example, the size of the group can be up to 100 persons.

4) Practical organisation

4.1 Leadership
- 1 co-ordinator sees that everything runs smoothly in the ladder tournament.

4.2 Organisation
- Look at the scoreboard to see which place has been alocated to you by lottery.
- Challenge a team (player) who is 1, 2, 3 or 4 places before you on the scoreboard or accept a challenge.
- When you have finished a game, put the equipment back where you found it.
- Try to avoid any disputes. Make the rules together to make the game playable.

4.3 Duration
2–4 hours.

4.4 Rules of the game

- When you are not playing, a challenge must always be accepted.
- The challenger decides which game will be played.
- If the challenger wins, the loser gets the challenger's place on the scoreboard.
- If the challenger loses (or the game is a draw), the position remains.
- A player may not challenge the same person successively.
- The winner of the challenge is the person who at the end of playing time – is at the top of the list on the scoreboard.
- Challenge a partner.
- Go on to the playing field.
- Test the game equipment before you start: for example, try to keep a flying object in the air for as long as possible.
- Decide together upon a form for the match by mutual agreement on the rules of the game – especially think about:

object of the game: – Way of returning the ball:
                               – with or without:
                                   – control stroke on the racket
                                 – interruption
                     – number of contacts per team
                     – etc.

scoring: – as in volleyball or table tennis or badminton or tennis etc.
serve: – the aim is to bring the ball into the game (overhand, underhand or both)
              – service location/place the service must land
              – 1 or 2 attempts
              – etc.

way of scoring: – longest set
                        – highest number of good attempts
                        – least (highest) number of "bad" ("good") points
                        – etc.

the partner's task: (double game)
             – obliged to play in turn or not
             – do not concentrate too long on one game, in order to make room for other players
             – look for other players and try other games and game equipment
             – a short description of each game should be available. This can be used as an aid but it is not obligatory.

5) Description of the games

The game number corresponds with the number on the field (cf. 6. organisational scheme).

5.1 Goal striking

Player A stays behind a line 4 m from the wall, bounces the ball and tries to throw the ball in a circle drawn on the wall.
Player B catches the ball, then bounces the ball and throws it into the circle.
Both players throw 10 times: the winner is the person who gets the ball into the circle the most times.

Errors: – throwing the ball outside the circle
           – standing on or over the 4 m line
Note: double game: 2 x 10 attempts.
(2 tennis rackets, 1 foam tennis ball, chalk)

5.2 Volley rally

The players stand behind the line about 3 m from the wall.
A player tries to make as long a volley rally as possible against the wall (the ball may not touch the ground).
Count the number of successive strikes: the longest set makes the winning score.
Each team has 4 attempts.
The team with the longest set is the winner.

Note: double game 2 x 2 attempts each
(2 tennis rackets, 1 foam tennis ball)

5.3 Hoop race

Player A bounces the ball into the hoop and tries to hit the ball into the hoop of player B.
Player B returns the ball (after bouncing) to the hoop of A.

Errors: – striking the ball out of the target area
             – bouncing the ball twice
Note: double game – play in turn
(2 hoops, 2 tennis rackets, 1 tennis ball)

5.4 Scoop volley

Using a scoop try to throw the ball over the net into the opponents' field.
After catching the ball you are not allowed to move anymore, you must remain at
that spot.

(1 badminton net, 2 scoops, 1 play-fit ball)

5.5 Tambourine ball

With a tambourine try to throw a table tennis ball, a play-fit ball (plastic ball with
holes), a foam ball or a plastic ball over the net into the opponents' field.
Follow the rules of volleyball with underhand service.

(2 tambourines, 1 play-fit ball, foam ball, table tennis ball or plastic ball, 1
badminton net)

5.6 Square tennis

Mini tennis in which the ball must be hit alternately into one square and then into
the other square (square 1 for the odd strikes, square 2 for the even strikes).

Note: Double game: each player stands in a square, places are changed when the
service is won.

(2 tennis rackets, 1 tennis ball, 1 net)

2	1
1	2

5.7 Badminton
Try to hit the shuttlecock with the racket over the net, into the opponents' field.
Serve from one of the service bases obliquely to the base of the opponent.

(2 badminton rackets, 1 shuttlecock, 1 badminton net)

5.8 Tebako
Serve from the point of the triangle into the opponents' triangle.
Follow tennis rules, except that the shuttlecock may not touch the ground.

(2 badminton rackets, 1 shuttle-cock, 1 net)

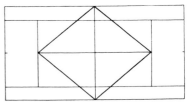

5.9 Swing tennis
Try to get the ball through the hole with one swing.
Both players have 10 attempts.

Note: In case of a doubles game, add the results of both players.
(1 old tennis racket in which a hole a little bit larger than a tennis ball has been made in the strings, 1 tennis ball + rope is attached to the strings)

5.10 Changing the bat

Table tennis rules with volleyball scoring system.
The players from each team must strike the ball alternately with bat 1 and then bat 2.

Note: In case of a doubles game each team uses one bat which should be passed back and forth between the players.
(1 table tennis table, 1 ball, 2 table tennis bats)

5.11 Family tennis

Family tennis is played with plastic rackets.
When serving, the ball should be dropped in the service area.
Tennis rules with volleyball scoring.

(2 plastic tennis rackets, 1 foam ball, 1 net)

5.12 Hand striking

Try to strike a shuttlecock (or foam ball) with the hand over the net into the field of the opponent(s).
Volleyball rules with underhand service.

(1 shuttlecock or foam ball, 1 net)

5.13 Wall table tennis

Player A serves by bouncing the ball on the table and then striking it on the bounce against the wall, above the line (at the height of the net).
Player B lets the ball bounce and strikes it back against the wall (above the line) so that (A) cannot strike it back.

Errors: – not being able to play the ball
back
– the ball bounces twice
– the ball does not bounce
– the ball touches (or is in) the
net

Note: In case of a doubles game, the players must strike the ball alternately.
(1/2 table tennis table, 2 table tennis bats, 1 ball)

5.14 Family table tennis

Play table tennis with a foam ball on 3 kitchen tables (see Floor table tennis: 5.17).

(3 kitchen tables, 1 foam ball, 2 table tennis bats)

5.15 Indiaca tennis

Tennis with a bat and an indiaca. The normal tennis rules apply with the exception that the indiaca may not touch the ground.

(2 bats, 1 indiaca, 1 net)

5.16 Play-fit badminton

Badminton with a play-fit ball. The purpose is to try to hit the ball with the racket over the net into the opponents' field. Serve from one of the service bases obliquely to the base of the opponent.

(2 badminton rackets, 1 play-fit ball, 1 net)

5.17 Floor table tennis

Try to throw the ball over the forbidden area into the opponents' field. If the opponent cannot play the ball back before it bounces a second time, you get 1 pt.
The forbidden area has the same function as the net.
To serve: the ball is bounced and then hit over the net.

(2 table tennis bats, 1 ball, chalk)

	forbidden area	

5.18 Rally

The ball has to be thrown above the line marked on the wall and must bounce before the dotted line marked on the ground.
Only the longest rally counts.
Each team has 3 attempts.
The team achieving the longest rally is the winner.

Note: For a doubles game, the ball is played alternately.
(2 tennis bats, 1 foam ball, chalk)

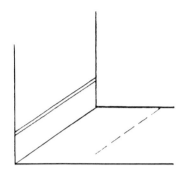

5.19 Jokari

Try to play as long a rally as possible.

(1 jokari, 1 tennis racket)

5.20 Hand tennis

A racket (without a handle) is attached to the hand (with rubber straps).
Try to hit the ball with the racket over the net into the opponents' field.
Use the normal volleyball rules with underhand service.

(2 old tennis rackets, 1 tennis ball, 1 net)

5.21 Mini tennis with control strike

The ball must be played with a control strike before striking it back.
If the ball can be stopped, run forward with it, throw it upwards and smash.
The service must land in the service area.

(2 tennis rackets, 1 tennis ball, 1 net)

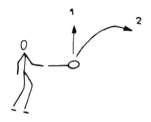

5.22 Dopp-ball

Hit the ball over the net towards the opponent with a two-handed strike using a dopp-ball bat.
The ball may not touch the ground.

(2 dopp-ball bats, 1 dopp-ball)

5.23 Wall squash

Player A tries to strike the ball against the wall in such a way that player B cannot strike the ball back before it bounces a second time.

service: – each player stays in their own service area
– the player who serves, hits the ball against the wall above the service line
– the rebounding ball must land in the service box of the opponent.

(2 squash rackets, 1 squash ball)

5.24 Scatch

Each player attaches a disc-shaped catching board to the catching hand.
Each player throws the scatch ball (a tennis ball with velcro) to the opponent.
The opponent tries to catch the ball with the catching board.

(2 catching boards, 1 scatch ball)

6) Organisational scheme

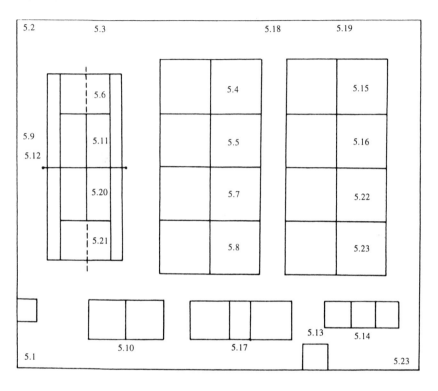

7) Equipment

– chalk or white tape	– 8 tennis paddles	– 2 squash rackets
– 7 foam tennis balls	– 2 hoops	– 2 play-fit balls
– 2 scoops	– 1 scoop ball	– 2 scatch catching boards
– 2 tambourines	– 2 squash balls	– 1 scatch ball
– 6 badminton rackets	– 2 shuttlecocks	– 2 table tennis tables
– 7 tennis rackets	– 4 tennis balls	– badminton net
– 3 old tennis rackets	– 1 indiaca	– 1 tennis net
– 6 table tennis bats	– 3 table tennis balls	– rope or elastic cord
– 3 kitchen tables	– 2 plastic tennis rackets	– 20 posts
– 1 badminton ball	– 1 jokari	
– 2 dopp-ball bats (2 bats)	– 1 dopp-ball (or tennis ball)	

10. Sports Tournament with Team Games

1) Activities and organisational form

A tournament with 9 team games for teams of 5-7 participants.
Finish with a group game.

2) Location

Soccer field (grass or hardened ground)
Beach (hard sand).

3) Target group

– young people, adults.

4) Practical organisation

4.1 Leadership
– 1 co-ordinator (scoreboard)
– 1 game leader per game (9 game leaders).

4.2 Organisation
– 18 teams with 5 to 7 players.
– System of promotion according to a designated scheme.

1st tour									
game	5.1	5.2	5.3	5.4	5.5	5.6	5.7	5.8	5.9
team	1	2	3	4	5	6	7	8	9
against	18	17	16	15	14	13	12	11	10

2nd tour									
game	5.1	5.2	5.3	5.4	5.5	5.6	5.7	5.8	5.9
team	9	1	2	3	4	5	6	7	8
against	17	16	15	14	13	12	11	10	18

- There are 9 rounds in total.
- Timing: 5 minutes explanation + practice
  10 minutes execution
  5 minutes to change – announcement of results.
- Field ribbons remain with the game.
- Scoring: game winner: 2 pts
  drawn score: 1 pt each.
- The team which scores the most points (up to 18) is the final winner.
- There is a captain per team who is responsible for passing the points to the coordinator and for following the scheme correctly (enclosed find a plastic map with the racing scheme).
- The fields are marked with field ribbons (rope, chalk lines, traffic cones or plastic bottles filled with water).

4.3 Duration
About 3 hours.

5) Description of the games

5.1 Castle ball
Playground
- a rectangle measuring about 20 m in length and 12 m in width
- 4 m from the width side (on both halves) there are circles (= castles) with a diameter of 4 m. Inside the circles there is a cone with a tennis ball on it.

Rules of the game
The player must knock over the opponents' castle with the balls. None of the players may step inside the circles. The team who has the ball must win the right of attack by playing the ball over the opponents' farside. This is a game of attack and defence of castles. The ball is played with the hands only. People may not run more than 3 steps with the ball. Dribbling is permitted.

(8 traffic cones, 2 tennis balls, 1 handball, chalk)

5.2 Quoits

Playground

Game area about 20 m x 10 m. A platform (box, cupboard, chair) is placed on both sides outside the playground at a distance of about 2 m. Each team has one player which stands on their plat-form with a stick in hand.

Rules of the game

By using teamwork, throw the ring on to your own player's stick. No running with the rings. No pulling the rings out of another's hands. On a free throw the players may not throw the ring straight on to the stick. Before throwing on to the stick players should have passed the ring at least 3 times. All players must catch and throw the ring with only one hand. When scoring: change the player with the stick (1 rubber ring (large), 2 wooden sticks, 2 raised platforms: e.g., chairs etc.)

5.3 Mini hockey

Playground

– length: 20-30 m, width: 12-15 m

– at both ends, in the middle there are 2 goals 2 m wide

– goal area: a half circle with a 4 m radius.

Rules of the game:
By using teamwork, the players try to hit the ball into the opponents' goal. Swinging the hockey stick above knee height is not allowed. The game leader must severely punish rough play. Always hold the stick with both hands. The keeper may touch the ball with the feet. The players must not step inside the goal area.

(12 hockey sticks (in a gym you could use a safe-t-play set or gymnastic sticks with gummy ring) 1 tennis ball, 2 mini soccer goals)

5.4 Four square indiaca
Playground
The field is divided into 4 squares. Each team splits up into 2 groups of 3 players and they stand in 2 opposite squares.

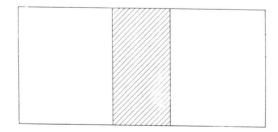

Rules of the game
Serve the indiaca with an underhand stroke. Try to make the indiaca land in one of the opponents' squares (cf. Volleyball). Each team has up to 3 hits (not obligatory!). Teamwork between the 2 squares is permitted.

Errors
– contact with the border lines
– hitting the ball out of the squares
– more than 3 successive touches
– the indiaca touches the ground in your own square.
(1 indiaca, 1 playground ribbon)

5.5 Volleyball without net
Playground
Length: 20-22 m, width: 9 m (if there are less than 12 players, the field can be shortened).

Rules of the game
The same rules as volleyball. The striped area = net: you must not step

inside this area and the ball must not bounce there. A smash is permitted. Under-hand service is required.

(4 Swedish benches or playground ribbon, 1 volleyball)

5.6 Strike ball

Playground

A rectangle 25 m in length and 20 m in width. Bases are positioned on each corner. The batter's box is placed 15 m from one of the sidelines. Between the fault lines, 5 m from the plate, a tipline is drawn. Exactly in the middle between bases 1 and 4, is the pitcher's mound.

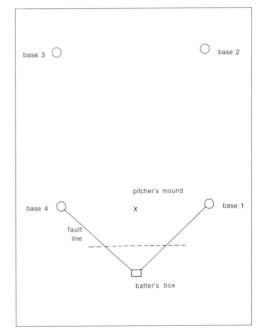

Rules of the game

One team is the batting team and is numbered. The other team are fielders and are positioned at the bases and at the pitcher's mound (x). The field player at the pitcher's mound throws a tennis ball underhand to the first batter.

The batter strikes the tennis ball with a bat or a cudgel into the field and runs around the bases 1, 2, 3 to 4. The field players try to stop the ball and play it to the pitcher. When the pitcher has the ball and is on the pitcher's mound, the game stops. If the runners are not on a base at that moment, they are out.

The runner may stop at any base. The player batting must strike the ball over the tipline, inside the fault lines and as far as possible (may hit further than bases 2 and 3).

When each player on the batting team has had a turn, they become the field team. Each team has one turn.

Score

Each runner who arrives on base 4 without being "out" gets 4 pts (each base = 1 pt). If the runner makes a home run, then they get 8 pts.

(4 bases, baseball bat, 1 tennis ball, 1 hoop)

5.7 Mini korfball

Playground
- length: 20-30 m;
  width: 12-15 m
- a korfball pole
  positioned in each
  half.

Rules of the game
The players use team-
work to put the ball in
the opponents' goal.
They may not run with the ball. There should be no body contact. The ball may be
held for only for a short time (maximum of 3 seconds).

(2 korfball poles + basket, 1 mini soccer ball)

5.8 Bucket ball

Playground
– a rectangle measuring about 20 m in length and 12 m in width.

Rules of the game
One player (keeper) stands at each of the two baselines on the field holding a
bucket. The keeper may move along this baseline. By making passes (running with
the ball is forbidden) the field players must try to put the ball in their own bucket.
The keeper may not touch the ball with the hands. The ball may only be held for a
short time (maximum of 3 seconds).

Errors
- rough play immediately gives a free throw: this means the opponents may play
  the ball to their own keeper from 8 m
- if the keeper touches the ball with the hands, it is a free throw for the other
  team.
- running with the ball is not permitted.
(2 buckets, 1 tennis ball)

5.9 Dice ball

Playground
– a basketball court or handball court
– in the mid-circle there is a cone with a large dice placed on it

Rules of the game
Same rules as handball. The goal is the backline. When team A puts the ball down behind team B's line, they obtain the right of attack the castle (= cone + dice). When the dice falls down, the number on top of the dice gives the amount of points. Nobody may enter the mid-circle.
(1 cone, 1 large dice, 1 basketball or handball court)

5.10 Swedish running game (the final game)

This is a kind of relay race where all the teams line up in the mid-circle on the soccer field. Each of the 18 teams has an answer sheet (see example below). Traffic cones are lined up around the soccer field, each with a large number.

On a signal (whistle, etc.), the first player from each team goes to the first number for that particular group. This number is visible from the starting position. The answer sheet and pencil must stay in the mid-circle of the soccer field. At each number there is a multiple choice question which must be answered (with a, b, c) at the starting place. After that, the next player runs to the next number, etc until one team has answered the whole list of questions.

Each correct answer gets 1 pt. The team which finishes first, gets 2 pts extra. The order indicated on the team list must be followed.

Swedish running game: team name:

number	answer
1	
2	
3	
4	
5	
6	
7	
8	
9	
10	
11	
12	
13	
14	
15	

(answer sheets, pencils, numbers, 15 cones, 15 multiple choice question lists, answer sheets)

6) Organisational scheme

7) Equipment

– 9 x 7 party ribbons	– 12 play-fit hockey sticks	– 1 mini soccer ball
– field ribbon	– 2 goals for mini soccer	– 2 buckets
– 24 traffic cones	– 1 indiaca	– 1 large dice
– 5 tennis balls	– 1 volleyball	– 4 bases
– 2 handballs	– 4 Swedish benches	– handball or basketball
– 1 rubber ring	– 1 hoop	– pencils + scoresheets
– 2 short sticks	– 1 bat	– scoreboard
– 2 chairs	– 2 korfball poles + basket	

– Swedish running game (20 question lists and answer sheets + numbers)

11. Table Tennis Tournament

1) Activities and organisational form

A varied group of table tennis games which are offered on a "come and go" basis in combination with a challenge system (pyramid).

2) Location

Sports hall.

3) Target group

- Due to the various games on offer, the group can be quite varied.

4) Practical organisation

4.1 Leadership
- 1 co-ordinator to maintain the organisation of the challenge system.

4.2 Organisation
- Look at your place in the pyramid. The starting position is determined by drawing lots.
- First of all, you have to beat somebody on the same row of the pyramid before you may challenge somebody from a higher row.
- The winner of the tournament is the person who at the end of the playing time is the highest on the pyramid.

4.3 Duration
2-4 hours.

4.4 General rules of the games
- Challenge a player or accept a challenge.
- Always accept a challenge when not playing.
- The challenger determines the game that will be played.

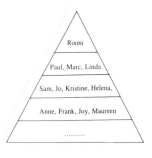

- If you win on the same row, challenge a higher row. If you win on a higher row, change places.
- If the challenger loses, the positions remain as they were before.
- Do not challenge the same person twice in succession.
- Look for a field.
- Try out the game first.
- Define the kind of game together with mutual agreements about the rules of the game.
  Think about:
  - the goal of the game (e.g., way of returning, number of touches)
  - scoring (table tennis or volleyball, etc.)
  - service (the purpose is to bring the ball into the game, where do you serve from and to? 1 or 2 tries?)
  - scoring (longest series? highest number of successful tries? fewest number of "bad" points?)
  - do not play one game for too long. Let other people play. Look for other people and try other games.
- A description of the game at each station serves as guide, but it is not binding.
- Once the pyramid tournament is over, some games may be played with the whole group.

5) Description of the games

The number of the game is the same as the number of the field (see 6. Organisational scheme).

5.1 Skill game
- Player A lays the ball on the bat and covers a fixed circuit marked out with 4 cones. The ball may not be touched with the hands. Count how many times the ball rolls off the bat.
- Each player has 2 tries.
- The winner is the player who lets the ball fall the least of times.

Note: This game can also be played in backhand or alternated between forehand and backhand.
(1 table tennis bat, 1 ball, 4 cones)

5.2 Quick touching
- Player A bounces the ball on the bat with a continuous forehand stroke.
- The exercise is executed for 1 minute.
- Each player has 2 tries.

- The winner is the player who can make the highest continuous number of bounces.

Note: This game can also be played backhand or alternated between forehand and backhand.

(1 table tennis bat, 1 ball, 1 stopwatch)

5.3 Wall striking
- Half of a table tennis table is placed against the wall.
- After the ball bounces, player A tries to hit the ball against the wall.
- The ball must bounce on the table again.
- Player B now hits the ball against the wall.
- If a mistake is made, the other player gets 1 pt.
- The winner is the player who reaches 10 pts first.

Errors: – hitting the ball against the wall, but failing to bounce the ball back on the table
    – not hitting the wall when a ball bounces back
    – letting the ball bounce twice.

(1/2 table tennis table, 1 ball, 2 table tennis bats, chalk)

5.4 Hitting targets
Same as 5.3 (Wall striking), but with a goal area drawn on the wall.

Errors: – hitting the ball out of the goal area
    – letting the ball bounce twice.

(1/2 table tennis table, 1 ball, 2 table tennis bats, chalk)

5.5 Square hitting
- Same as 5.3 (Wall striking), but squares are drawn on the wall.
- Each player hits the ball in turn.
- For every hit in a square (or on the line), the player gets 1 pt.
- The ball may also be returned without bouncing on the table first.
- Winner is the first player who has 21 pts.

(1/2 table tennis table, 1 ball, 2 table tennis bats, chalk)

5.6 Floor table tennis
- Draw a table tennis field with chalk on the floor and in the middle of it stretch a rope or a net between 2 little poles (about 15 cm in height).
- The players play sitting down and apply the normal table tennis rules.
- You play up to 10 pts.

(2 little poles + net, 2 table tennis bats, 1 ball, chalk)

5.7 Trench table tennis
- The 2 halves of the table are 30-50 cm apart and you play without a net.
- Play by the normal table tennis rules.
- Play up to 10 pts.
(1 table tennis table, 1 ball, 2 table tennis bats)

5.8 Mini table tennis
- Play on 1/2 table tennis table. The net is put in the middle of the half table.
- Play up to 10 pts.
- Play by the normal table tennis rules.
(1/2 table tennis table, 1 ball, 2 table tennis bats, 1 net)

5.9 Corner table tennis
- Place the 2 half tables diagonally to each other.
- Play up to 10 pts.
- Play by the normal table tennis rules.
(1 table tennis table, 1 ball, 2 table tennis bats)

5.10 Collecting points
- On each half table 3 squares are drawn (worth 1, 2, or 3 pts).
- Each time the ball hits the square (or hits the line) it is worth the number of points for that square.
- The winner is the player who reaches 21 pts first.
- Play by the normal table tennis rules.
(1 table tennis table, 1 net, 1 ball, 2 table tennis bats)

5.11 Volley table tennis
- On the ground a field is drawn about 10 x 5 m and a net is placed in the middle of the field at a height of about 1.5 m.
- Play the ball directly over the net.
- Play according to volleyball rules.
- Play up to 10 pts.
(2 poles + badminton net, 2 table tennis bats, 1 ball, chalk)

5.12 Group game: Chinese table tennis
- The players are divided into 2 groups, each group is placed at opposite sides of the table.
- The first player hits the ball to the opposite side and queues up at the opposite side of the table.

- If a player misses a ball or does not hit the table, they must leave the game.
- The winner is the player who remains at the end of the game.

(1 table tennis table, 1 ball, 1 net, 4 table tennis bats)

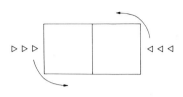

6) Organisational scheme

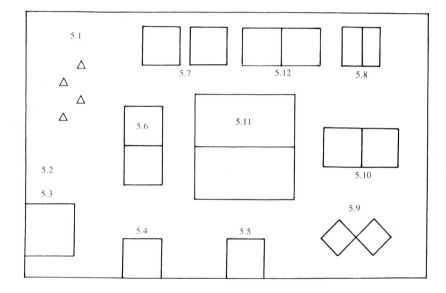

7) Equipment

- 6 table tennis tables (12 halves)
- 4 table tennis nets
- 12 table tennis balls
- 2 poles
- 20 table tennis bats
- 1 badminton net
- 1 stopwatch

- 4 cones
- name boards
- rope
- large paper with a pyramid on it
- 2 little poles
- chalk

12. Recreational Tennis Tournament

1) Activities and organisational form

Tennis tournament in which many participants may play in a short time.

A combination of the "group"-system and "free for all".

Note: This form of tournament can also be used for table tennis and badminton.

2) Location

Sports hall (2 tennis courts).

3) Target group

– young people from 12-18
– tennis players
– this example has been worked out for a group of about 32 players.

4) Practical organisation

4.1 Leadership
- 1 general co-ordinator (to see that all goes well, monitor the scoreboard)
- 8 game leaders (1 game leader per half tennis court).

4.2 Organisation
- Put the names of the participants in a box; then pull out the names in pairs.
- The pairs are divided into 4 groups.
- Each tennis court is divided into 4 mini courts.
- Each game leader is responsible for 1 mini court.
- Each game leader keeps the score for his/her own field and gives the points to the co-ordinator.
- At the moment that the winners of the 4 groups play against each other, a free for all tennis match is prepared on the empty court (choose games from the tennis circuit, see pages 81-86).

4.3 Duration
Half a day.

5) Description of the games

- Per group, each pair plays against another pair.

group 1	group 2	group 3	group 4
A – B	E – F	I – J	M – N
C – D	G – H	K – L	O – P
A – C	E – G	I – L	M – P
B – D	H – F	K – J	O – N
A – D	E – H	I – K	M – O
B – C	F – G	J – L	N – P

- The winners of each group play against each other.

    final round:
        winner group 1 – winner group 2
        winner group 3 – winner group 4
        winner group 1 – winner group 3
        winner group 4 – winner group 2
        winner group 1 – winner group 4
        winner group 2 – winner group 3

- Ranking from places 1 to 4.
- "Tie-break" matches are played. In the "tie-break" game, count the points. The first player who has 7 pts wins the game.

6 Organisational scheme

For the "tennis free for all", use field "A".

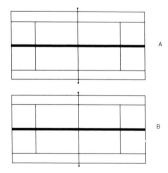

7) Equipment

- 8 moveable nets or 4 wide elastic lines   – 8 tennis balls
- 8 posts   – 32 tennis rackets
- material for "free for all" tennis (depends on the games chosen)

13. Recreational Badminton Tournament

1) Activities and organisational form

A badminton tournament at which many participants can play in a short time. The winner of the tournament is the "emperor".

Note: This form of tournament can also be used for table tennis and tennis.

2) Location

Sports hall.

3) Target group

- Young people from 12-18
- Badminton players
- The circuit is designed for a group of about 20 players.

4) Practical organisation

4.1 Leadership

- 1 general co-ordinator (to see all goes well)
- 3 game leaders (1 game leader per 2 courts).

4.2 Organisation

- There is a number on each half of the badminton court.
- By drawing lots, the participants get a number; they go to the court with that number.
- Doubles matches are played.
- Each match lasts 15 minutes.
- Each match starts when the whistle is blown.
- The match ends after the second whistle. In case of a draw, the players must play on until there is a 1 pt difference.
- The participants have 2 minutes between matches to change courts.

4.3 Duration

Half a day.

5) Description of the tournament

- Each game starts at the same time on all the courts.
- A coin toss-up determines who may start serving.
- After every 5 pts, the service is changed.
- When the whistle is blown, all players who have won (who have the most points) move one field over to the left, to a half court marked with an odd number.
- The losers will move across to the right, to the half court with the even numbers.
- The winner is the pair who at the end of the tournament are at the far left (this is the "emperor's" place).

6) Organisational scheme

E = emperor   W = winner   L = loser   R = reserve

If there are not enough badminton courts, there may be several reserve players. After each whistle signal, 2 reserve players start at the extreme right of the field, the field with the odd numbers. The players who lose at the extreme right field become reserve players.

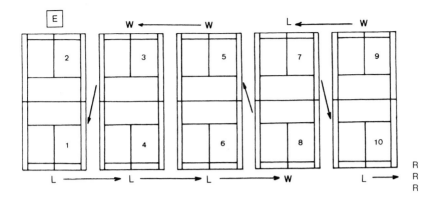

7) Equipment

- stopwatch   - 5 badminton nets
- chalk   - 5 shuttlecocks
- 10 posts   - papers with numbers (= number of participants for drawing lots)

14. Recreational Soccer Tournament

1) Activities and organisational form

Soccer tournament which allows all the players to play at the same time.

2) Location

Soccer field.

3) Target group

- young people from 12-18
- soccer players
- the circuit is worked out for a group of maximum 50 players.

4) Practical organisation

4.1 Leadership

- 1 co-ordinator
- 5 game leaders (1 per field).

4.2 Organisation

- The soccer field is divided into 5 small fields.
- Per game field there are 5 ribbons to separate the teams.
- Each half field has a board with a letter on it.
- Each player draws lots to determine on which field the player will play soccer.
- All the players' names are put in a game schedule, which determines on which field they have to play (indicated by a letter).
- 5 matches are played with 4 against 4 or with 5 against 5, depending on the number of participants.
- Each match takes 10 minutes. Between matches, 5 minutes are provided to allow the players to change fields.
- A whistle is blown at the start and end of each match.
- The co-ordinator explains to the participants:
  - *   how to read the schedule
  - *   how to obtain points
  - *   the rules of the game
  - *   start and ending whistle signals
  - *   how to change fields
- After the explanation the co-ordinator gives a general warm up.
- After the warm up the first match begins.

4.3 Game scheme

name player	match 1		match 2		match 3		match 4		match 5		total pts	final result
	field n°	pts	field n°	pts	field n°	pts	field n°	pts	field n°	pts		

4.4 Duration

Half a day.

5) Description of the games

The players look at the game schedule to find out where (which field half) they will start. The game leaders give ribbons to one team and at the whistle signal, the first match will start. Now the game leader is referee. After 10 minutes a second whistle signal indicates the end of the first match.

            win   = 20 pts
            draw   = 10 pts
            lose   = 0 pts

The goals scored are added to the points obtained.
Example: Mary's team won by 4-3; they get 24 pts.
                     Bram's team lost the match, but made 3 goals, they get 3 pts.

At the end of each match, the game leader writes the score on a form which is given to the co-ordinator.

        match 1 result   points
        A - B   4 - 3   A = 24 pts
                             B =   3 pts

Meanwhile, by drawing lots, the co-ordinator has indicated on the game scheme on which field each player will play the second match. The players go to the field for the second match and at the whistle the second match is started. The co-ordinator fills in the points for each player on the game schedule. When the 5 matches have been played, the points are added up per player and the end result is determined.

6) Organisational scheme

– division of the soccer field.

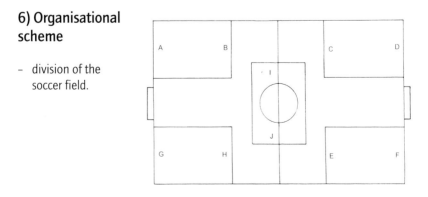

field division

The division of the field depends on the number of participants.
Example for 47 participants.

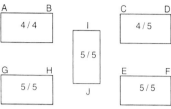

Example for 49 participants.

Example for 35 participants.

7) Equipment

- 10 mini goals
- 5 soccer balls
- 25 ribbons
- 10 boards with letters (A - J)
- large game schedule
- name boards

- whistle
- fill-in forms
- tape
- stopwatch
- marker pens

15. Recreational Korfball Tournament

1) Activities and organisational form

A playing card tournament which allows players to play in a team unit, in which they can participate in different kinds of korfball games in short time periods.

2) Location

Soccer field.

3) Target group

- young people from 12-18
- korfball players.

4) Practical organisation

4.1 Leadership
- 1 co-ordinator
- 3 game leaders (1 per field).

4.2 Organisation
-   The soccer field is divided into 3 fields.

- The participants are divided into 4 groups by means of playing cards: hearts, diamonds, clubs and spades.
- Each group has at least 20 participants.
- Each team has a captain who ensures that the correct number of players for the team are on the right field for the competition.
- A different game is played on each field.
- At the end, the captains give the points for their team to the co-ordinator.
- There are 5 rounds and each round lasts 20 minutes.
- There is a rest time of 10 minutes between each round.

4.3 Duration
About 3 hours.

5) Description of the games

5.1 Mono korfball
2 teams play against each other. There are 4 players from each team on the field. They play korfball according to the rules of 1 section korfball. Each team plays against another team for 1 round.

scoring: The team with the most goals gets 2 pts.
The team with the least goals gets 1 pt.
(2 korfball poles + basket, 1 soccer ball).

5.2 Micro korfball
2 teams play against each other. There are 8 players from each team on the field - 4 defenders and 4 attackers. Play according to the rules of micro korfball (2 section korfball). Each team plays another team for 1 round.

scoring: The team with the most goals gets 2 pts.
The team with the least goals gets 1 pt.
(2 korfball poles + basket, 1 soccer ball).

5.3 Field korfball
2 teams play against each other. There are 12 players from each team on the field - 4 players in each section. Play according to the rules of field korfball (3 section korfball). Each team plays against another team for 1 round.

scoring: The team with the most goals gets 2 pts.
The team with the least goals gets 1 pt.
(2 korfball poles + basket, 1 soccer ball).

6) Organisational scheme

on field 1: mono korfball
on field 2: micro korfball
on field 3: field korfball

H = hearts   D = diamonds   C = clubs   S = spades   M.P. = meeting place

field 1:	Field 2:	Field 3:
H – S	D – C	H – S
D – C	H – S	C – D
H – C	D – S	H – C
D – S	H – C	D – S
H – D	S – C	D – H
S – C	H – D	S – C

M.P.H.   **1**   **2**   **3**   M.P.D.

M.P.C.   M.P.S.

7) Equipment

– scoreboard	– 6 soccer balls	– field rope
– playing cards	– 6 korfball poles and baskets	– stopwatch

RECREATIONAL ORGANISATION SET-UPS

16. Swimming on a "Come and Go" Basis

1) Activities and organisational form

A range of swimming and water games on a "come and go" basis.
The participants themselves choose which games they play or they are cheered on or invited by the team leaders to do so.

2) Location

Swimming pool (indoor or open air).

3) Target group

- principally for children but adults can also participate
- for swimmers as well as for non-swimmers.

4) Practical organisation

4.1 Leadership
- 1 general co-ordinator
- 2 managers for the reception desk
    a) changing rooms
    b) entrance swimming hall
    – show the participants where to go
    – check the participants swimming skills:
      participants who can swim get a white bathing cap
      participants who can not swim get a green bathing cap
- 6 game leaders
  tasks: set up the material, supervision, encouragement (it is advisable to allocate 1 leader per 3 to 4 games depending on whether the game needs instructors or not)
- all game leaders wear the same T-shirt.

4.2 Organisation
A sign should indicate the name for each game. The non-swimmers are directed to the shallow end.

Accessories: music; decoration of the swimming hall; first aid; refreshments; side activities.

Placement of the activities
The activities should be placed in such a way that:
- One activity is not in the way of another.
- There is enough room to walk by and to observe the activity.
- The whole activity remains visible.
- There is possibility for variation or change: if you realise that a set-up is not very good, you should be able to change it.

Equipment
- The material must be easily visible and available at different games so that the participants see it as an invitation.
- The equipment must be:
    - Inviting and colourful
    - Of a good quality (e.g., waterproof, strong)
    - Safe (e.g., tyre valves must be eliminated)
    - Sufficient in number and universal so that everybody recognises the activity very quickly.
    - It is desirable to make an inventory of the equipment used and give it to the activity leaders, so that they can make sure that everything is returned.

4.3 Duration
Set up: 1 hour
Programme: about 2 1/2 hours
Clean up: 1/2 hour.

5) Description of the games

5.1 Get the horn
Tie a piece of elastic around each participant and attach it to the side of the pool. Swim against the resistance of the elastic line up to the horn that is attached to a rope on a stick.
(1 tyre, 1 elastic line,
stick, 1 rope, 1 horn)

5.2 Broom race

Run holding a filled bucket placed on a kickboard, around the buoy in the pool.

(2 sticks + kickboard + plastic bucket, buoy)

5.3 Swim till the end

Two tyres are tied together with an elastic line and float in the middle of the swimming pool. By 2's, each participant gets into a tyre and tries to swim to the opposite end. The goal is to reach the opposite end as quickly as possible.

(2 tyres with an elastic line per pair)

5.4 Skippy ball

A circuit of cones is made on the side of the pool. Cover that circuit bouncing on a skippy ball.

(cones + skippy ball)

5.5 Form of crossing

An elastic line is stretched over the width of the swimming pool. Everybody sitting on a raft must use the elastic line to pull themselves to the side.

(raft, elastic line)

5.6 Wrestle island

A big mountain is made out of tyres in the middle of the swimming pool. Try to reach the top of the tyre mountain.

(20 car tyres, elastic line, 3 anchoring boards)

5.7 Treasure diving

Diving for all kind of materials such as: word boards, numbers, balls, etc.
(diving materials)

5.8 Running mat

Running, rolling, etc. on the mat.
(running mat + material to attach it)

5.9 Keeper

The keeper throws a ball. Each participant tries to catch the ball and make a goal in the (water)polo goal.
(4 beach balls, goal)

5.10 Basket goaling

Throw the ball from the edge of the pool to somebody in the water. This person tries to throw the ball into the basketball hoop which is on the side of the pool.
(4 beach balls, 1 basketball hoop)

5.11 Table tennis

Normal table tennis played at the side of the pool, not in the water.
(table tennis table, 1 ball, 4 table tennis bats)

5.12 Shovelboard

Play shovelboard at the side of the pool.
(1 shovelboard + disks)

5.13 Jumping circus

Jump from the edge of the pool into the water in different ways, with and without hoops.
(5 hoops)

5.14 Parachute jumping

Jump with a plastic bag from the diving board. Hold the plastic bag as a parachute over your head.
(dustbin bags)

5.15 Tyre throwing

Score points by throwing a ball from the sides of the pool into tyres floating in the water.
(10 balls + 10 numbered tyres)

5.16 Fishing match

Dive for coloured transparent material on the bottom of the pool, cut out fishes and stick them on the windows of the swimming pool so that it looks like an aquarium.
(5 pairs of scissors, model fish, coloured plastic paper)

5.17 Clumsy driver

Sit on a horizontal kick board and paddle with your hands round a buoy and back to the starting point.
(4 kick boards, 1 buoy)

5.18 Fire engine

Put a cup on a cone (right side up). Push the cone down in the water and shoot the cups away as high as possible.
(4 cones, 8 plastic cups)

5.19 Little Tom Thumb

Cross the swimming pool with large rubber boots, relay style.
(3 pairs of clean rubber boots)

5.20 Mail coach

In a half plastic barrel, paddle with your hands to the other side of the pool as quickly as possible.
(2 plastic half barrels)

5.21 Running mat

Same as 5.8. (Running mat) but in the shallow end (for those who cannot swim).
(running mat + material to attach it)

5.22 Recreation ground

All kind of things are placed in the swimming pool and the participants play with the toys.
(balls, tyres, raft, etc.)

5.23 Swedish swimming game

Answer plastic-coated questions which are hanging around the swimming pool.
Note: There is the possibility of finishing this with a group game.

For example

Whirlpool: All participants form a circle, they run around (making a whirlpool) and then let themselves float away from the centre.

6) Organisational scheme

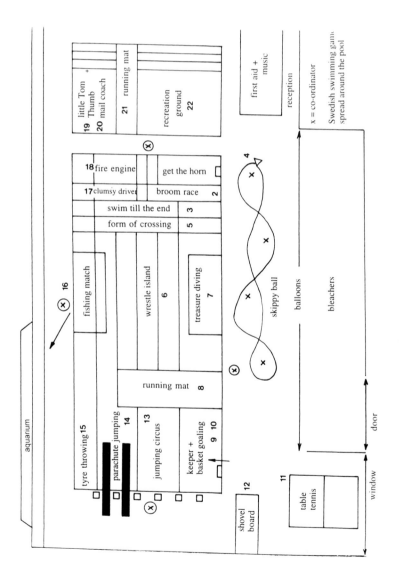

7) Equipment

- large floor plan
  (placing the equipment)
- music boxes
- balloons
- 4 table tennis bats
- 14 tyres (car) + 5 numbered tyres
- 10 tyres (truck)
- 10 elastic lines
- 1 horn or bell
- 3 sticks + platform
- beach and water toys (for children)
- 1 shovelboard + disks
- 15 fixing plates
- 20 cones
- diving items
- 20 beach balls
- kitchen tables

- numbers + description
  of the games + drawings
- 1 table tennis ball
- 1 movable net for table tennis
- 1 table tennis table
- 10 hoops
- 10 short sticks
- 10 dustbin bags
- 3 pairs of rubber boots
- 1 basket
- rope
- 2 buckets
- 4 skippy balls
- 4 rafts
- 2 running mats
- Swedish swimming game
  (questions in plastic cover)

17. Cycling Tour

1) Activities and organisational form

A (tourist) cycling circuit in combination with a certain number of cycling skills and exercises.

2) Location

At best you can follow an existing tourist route or another fixed circuit on quiet roads.
Cycling games and circuit: – parking lot or recreation area
                              – school playground.

3) Target group

– for children (about 12 years) as well as for adults.

4) Practical organisation

4.1 Leadership
- 1 group leader
- 1 person in the follow-up car, who stays behind the last cyclist, provides assistance if needed, and warns other traffic on the road
- 1 coach in front with a leading car (or motorcycle) if a public road is used.

4.2 Organisation
– Reservation of bicycles + other items.

In advance:
- Check the materials.
- Arrange for extra equipment + repair material.

- Make detailed arrangements about:
    - the route to follow
    - special plans in case there are accidents on the way
    - regulations about cycling in a group
    - cycling technique
    - drinks + lunch (e.g., reservations made in a café along the way)
    - information about the cycling route
    - possible information about things worth seeing along the way.

4.3 Duration
Total time (with lunch) about 4 hours.

5) Description of the games

- cycling route of about 40 km
- halfway: resting place (lunch)
- cycling game + cycling skills circuit at the end of the route.

5.1 The longest time
All the cyclists form a single file; try to co-ver the distance between 2 lines as slowly as possible (about 5 m).

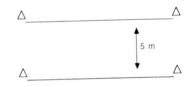

Rules of the game
- Touching the ground with the feet is forbidden.
- No use of brakes.
- The cyclist can go maximum 1 m to the left and to the right.
(chalk, 4 cones)

5.2 Steal the cones
At the signal, the 2 teams try to move the cones behind their own line as quickly as possible.

Rules of the game
- Touching the ground is prohibited, if a foot touches the ground you must start again.

- It is forbidden to hinder your opponent.
- You can only move 1 cone at a time.
- Throwing cones is forbidden.
(chalk, 24 cones)

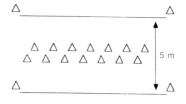

5.3 Steal the cones (with obstacles)
Same as 5.2 (Steal the cones), but there is only 1 row with cones.

Rules of the game:
- Touching the ground is prohibited.
- You can only take 1 cone at once.
- Throwing the cones is forbidden.
- Hindering your opponent is allowed.
(chalk, 14 cones)

5.4. Cycling skills circuit
Part A

1. Start: 1 foot on the pedal, 1 foot on a box.
2. Slalom between the cones.
3. Cycle between narrow boards placed on the ground.
4. Cycle around the cone.
5. Cycle over the beam.
6. Cycle and take a bottle placed on a chair (with the left hand).
7. Cycle round the cone and put the bottle in your right hand.
8. Cycle between the cones, put the bottle back on the chair.
9. Cycle over a slanted plane of wood and around the cone.

Part B
10. Put the bicycle on the ground, take 5 balls and throw them in the basket behind the marked line (all the balls must go in the basket!).

Part C
11. Get back on the bicycle and ride over a balancing board.
12. Ride between the funnel shaped boards.
13. Finish: standing between the boxes with 1 foot on the pedal and 1 foot on a box.

Errors: If a foot touches the ground in Part A or C, the exercise must be started
            again.

Who makes the best time?
(4 boxes, 15 cones, 4 narrow boards, 2 wide boards, 1 beam, 2 chairs, 1 bottle, 5
tennis balls, 1 basket, 1 slanted plane of wood)

6) Organisational scheme

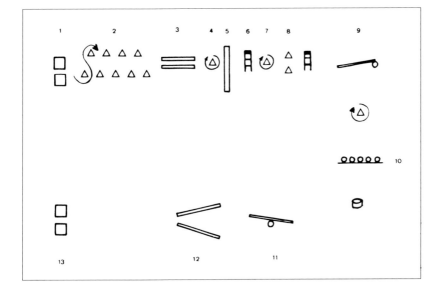

7) Equipment

- 1 bicycle per participant
- spare tyres + bicycle repair kits
- walkie-talkies if possible
- 24 cones
- 4 narrow boards (about 3 m)
- 4 boxes
- 2 wide boards (30 x 80 cm)
- card marked with the cycling route
  or an ordonance map
- 1 basket
- chalk
- 5 tennis balls
- 1 bottle
- 2 chairs
- 1 slanted plane (80 cm wide)
- 1 beam

18. Double Orientation

1) Activities and organisational form

An orientation game for groups where some skills tasks must be executed.

2) Location

Anywhere possible.

3) Target group

– children and adults.

4) Practical organisation

4.1 Leadership
– 1 co-ordinator
– 10 coaches (1 per game).

4.2 Organisation
–   Groups of 6 players. Each group receives a scoresheet + pencil in a plastic cover (to be placed around the neck of the captain).
–   All the groups start with game 1. After finishing that game, the captain goes to the co-ordinator and throws 2 dice; the sum of the dice indicates the place where the group must go to next.
–   There the group executes the next test, the score is noted and the captain throws the dice again, etc.

Rules of the game
–   When the dice indicate a game you have already executed, you receive a penalty (15 seconds).
–   If you throw 12, the group must wait for 2 minutes and then the captain throws again.

4.3 Scoresheet

Group:

TO	GAME TIME	PENALTIES	TOTAL
train race			
bench relay race			
"ski" running			
skippy ball race			
comb. relay race			
towel ball			
hockey slalom			
stilt walking			
bag running			
twins soccer			
running blind			

Total time:

4.4 Duration
About 2 hours.

5) Description of the games

5.1 Train race
The first player in each group runs around a cone (distance of 10 m), comes back and hooks arms with player 2. Both run to the cone, round the pin and back, and then hook arms with player 3 etc.
When all the players have run, the first player drops out and the remaining 5 run around the cone, etc.. Player 2 drops out etc.

Note: 2 groups execute this game at the same time.
(2 cones)

5.2 Bench relay race
With the help of Swedish benches (or boards) you must cover a distance between 2 lines (about 15 m). The players are not allowed to touch the floor.
(2 benches)

5.3 "Ski" running

With the help of 2 "skis" you must cover a distance (2 x 5 m) up and down and around the cone.

(2 boards with straps to attach to feet, 1 cone)

5.4 Skippy ball race

3 skippy balls are tied to each other with an elastic line (1 m long). The first 3 players bounce for 10 m up to and around a cone then back again (10 m); after this, the next 3 players go.

(3 skippy balls, 1 elastic line, 1 cone)

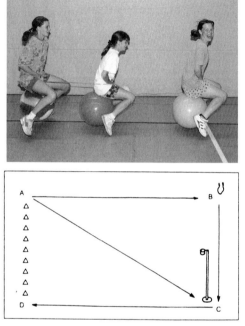

5.5 Combination relay race

Starting at "A", roll the ball across to "C", run to "B", skip 10 times, run to "C", take the ball, shoot it into the basket, dribble to "D", slalom between the cones to "A". Then the next player begins.

(6 cones, 1 skipping rope, 1 korfball pole + basket, 1 soccer ball)

5.6 Towel ball

The players hold a towel (in pairs). The first pair throws the ball to the next group using their towel. This group tries to catch the ball using the towel. In this way the 3 groups try to cover a fixed distance. If the ball falls, start again at the place where it was thrown from the last time.

(3 towels, 1 volleyball)

5.7 Hockey slalom

On the field a circuit of cones is set out. Player 1 starts, guides a tennis ball with a hockey stick around the circuit and passes the hockey stick to player 2, etc.

(10 cones, 1 hockey stick, 1 tennis ball)

5.8 Stilt walking

On the field an obstacle circuit is set out. Player 1 starts on stilts, covers the circuit and passes the stilts to player 2. If, during the circuit, a player steps off the stilts, they must redo the last obstacle again and will get 1 penalty point.

(2 stilts, 4 hoops, 10 cones)

5.9 Gunny sack running

Player 1 starts at the line holding the gunny sack, skips to the cone, rounds the cone, skips back to the starting line and passes the sack to the next player, etc.

(1 gunny sack, 1 cone)

5.10 Twins soccer

1 pair of the players' legs are tied together. The first pair dribbles the ball by foot between the cones. At the last cone, they shoot to score. The pair takes the ball and runs back with it to the second pair. The group must make 5 goals in total.

(1 elastic line, 6 cones, 1 soccer ball, 1 mini soccer goal)

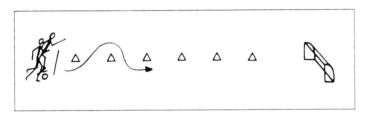

5.11 Running blind

All the players queue up and hold the shoulders of the player in front. The players are blindfolded except for the last one. On the field, a circuit is set out with cones. The last player must lead the whole group, without talking. They can indicate how the group must walk by pinching the shoulder of the player in front. The pinches are relayed from player to player up to the first player.
1 pinch on the right shoulder = go to the right
1 pinch on the left shoulder = go to the left
1 pinch on both shoulders = go straight on
2 pinches on both shoulders = stop

(6 towels, 6 cones)

6) Organisational scheme

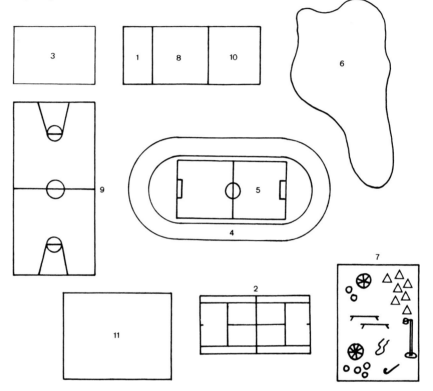

	Place	Game
1.	secretary's office	train race
2.	tennis field	bench relay race
3.	parking lot	"ski" running
4.	athletic track	skippy ball race
5.	soccer field	combination relay race
6.	lawn	towel ball
7.	recreation ground	hockey slalom
8.	café	stilt walking
9.	basketball court	gunny sack running
10.	sports hall	twins soccer
11.	playing field	running blind

7) Equipment

- 1 scoresheet + pencil per group
- 10 stopwatches (1 per coach)
- 2 Swedish benches (or boards)
- 3 skippy balls
- 2 soccer balls
- 1 skipping rope
- 1 tennis ball
- 1 gunny sack
- 1 volleyball
- 2 "skis"
  (board + straps to attach to the feet)

- 20 dice (2 per coach)
- 42 cones
- elastic line
- 4 hoops
- 1 korfball pole + basket
- 1 hockey stick
- 2 stilts
- 9 towels
- 1 mini soccer goal

19. Triathlon

1) Activities and organisational form

An endurance test derived from the triathlon and adapted to the different age groups.

The tests are:
- swimming
- cycling
- running

2) Location

Swimming pool and athletic t rack.

3) Target group

- young people from 15-20

4) Practical organisation

4.1 Leadership
- 1 co-ordinator
- 9 timers
- 2 secretary managers
- 4 coaches (for the different age groups)
- 3 referees

4.2 Organisation
- The participants are divided into groups
  Group 1 = 15-16-17 years
  Group 2 = 18-19-20 years
- The time in each separate test is considered and is counted. The 3 times are added together. The winner is the participant with the lowest total time. A ranking is made per group.
- If there are lots of participants, you can work under 2 systems:
  a) passing system: the order of the tests is not the same for all the participants
  b) working with sub-groups, which after the first test do the second (this system requires plenty of time).

4.3 Duration
Half a day (depends on the number of participants).

5) Description of the games

5.1 Swimming
Group 1 (15-17 years)
    girls   150 m
    boys   200 m

Group 2 (18-20 years)
    girls   200 m
    boys   250 m

5.2 Cycling
Group 1 (15-17 years)   Group 2 (18-20 years)
    girls   2,000 m   girls   3,000 m
    boys   3,000 m   boys   4,000 m

5.3 Running
Group 1 (15-17 years)   Group 2 (18-20 years)
    girls   1,200 m   girls   1,600 m
    boys   1,600 m   boys   2,000 m

6) Organisational scheme

- swimming (swimming pool)
- cycling (outside the athletics ring)
- running (inside the athletics ring)

7) Equipment

- about 20 stopwatches
- pencils
- scoreboard
- 20 bicycles

- players' numbers or coloured participation cards to note the time
- 3 starting pistols
- rope to indicate the circuit

20. Circuit: Living Game of Goose

1) Activities and organisational form

The game of goose is taken as a starting point for a circuit of tasks. The route is marked with numbered signs. The route is a closed circle so you can use different points to start and many teams can start at the same time. The teams toss a dice and move along the route of the number shown. When the team arrives at a coloured number, they complete a task. The starting number of the team is also the ending number.

2) Location

Sports hall, forest, open space.

3) Target group

- young people from 12-18
- can also be played with adults.

4) Practical organisation

4.1 Leadership
- As many game leaders as there are teams, or as many game leaders as there are tasks.

4.2 Organisation
- Make teams of 8-10 people.
- The route should be marked with 100 numbers.
- The numbers with a task are coloured, the others are black. The description of the task is with the number.
- When the team arrives at a number with a task, it should be executed. The game leader checks. When the task is accomplished, the team tosses the dice again and goes to the number shown.

4.3 Duration
Half a day.

5) Description of the tasks

N° 1:   Make an original pyramid with the team.

N° 4:   The whole team skips rope for 2 minutes (2 people turn a large rope).

N° 7:   By 2: With the right hand, take the left leg of a partner. Bend your right leg 5 times.

N° 10: Make a centipede: each player puts his/her legs on the shoulders of the player behind and leans with only hands on the ground. Try to cover a specific distance in this way.

N° 16: By 2: sit on each others' knees in a circle. Make 5 steps forwards, 5 steps backwards. Lie down and then stand up again.

N° 17: 20 push-ups.

N° 21: Arms stretched forward, each player makes a pinching action with the hands 50 times (open and close, where the fingers are completely stretched).

N° 22: By 2: do a handstand on the partner's feet and go forward 4 m.

N° 36: By 2: back to back, go forward (about 10 m).

N° 38: Cossack dance for 1 minute.

N° 39: Do 40 sit-ups.

N° 42: Do 30 knee bends and knee stretches.

N° 43: All the players queue up and hold the shoulders of the player in front. The players are blindfolded except for the last one. On the field, a circuit is set out with cones. The last player must lead the whole group, without talking.

Only by pinching the shoulder of the player in front of him, can they indicate how the group must walk. The pinches are relayed from player to player up to the first player.

1 pinch on the right shoulder = go to the right
1 pinch on the left shoulder = go to the left
1 pinch on both shoulders = go straight on
2 pinches on both shoulders = stop
(8-10 towels or blindfolds, 6 cones)

N° 45: By 2: A sits with legs spread apart; B stands with legs together; B jumps and spreads legs in the air the same time as A is closing his/her legs. Do this 20 times each and then change places.

N° 52: By 3: B stands behind A. Together they lift C, with C's feet on A's shoulders and hands on B's shoulders they walk forwards 10 m.

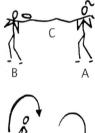

N° 58: Throw the ball upwards and catch it behind you with both hands between the legs. Each player needs 2 successful attempts.
(1 ball)

N° 61: By 2: back to back, in a "chair" position, sit still for 30 seconds.
(1 stopwatch)

N° 63: By 2: sit back to back, (as above), stand up and sit down again 10 times.

N° 67: 1 person sits on one end of a Swedish bench, the others are lined up behind each other. Each participant lifts the other end of the Swedish benchoverhead and puts it down on the other side. (1 bench)

N° 72: In the group play an indiaca 30 x from hand to hand.
(1 indiaca)

N° 81: One person plays "dead". The other persons lift him/ her into a handstand (4 group members play "dead").

N° 84: By 2: A makes a bridge, B goes under it. A lies down, B jumps over A.
Repeat this 3 times and change.

N° 87: 3 players juggle 3 balls for 2 minutes.
(3 balls)

N° 88: Execute 4 head springs with or without help.

N° 90: Everybody lines up one behind the other and takes the foot of the person ahead. In this way a specified distance should be followed while skipping

N° 93: Throw 10 tennis balls into a bucket from a specified distance.
(1 bucket, 10 tennis balls)

N° 97: Twins soccer: holding hands by 2. Starting with the ball on the cone (10 m from the goal). Make 10 goals together. After each goal, start at the cone again.
(1 cone, 1 soccer ball, 2 poles + rope)

6) Equipment

- 5 balls
- 1 stopwatch
- 1 indiaca
- 10 tennis balls
- 1 bucket

- 3 cones
- 8 bandages
- 2 poles
- chalk
- rope

21. Public Games Afternoon

1) Activities and organisational form

Public games in small groups following a free choice programme.

2) Location

Sports hall or open space.

3) Target group

- children as well as adults can participate.

4) Practical organisation

4.1 Leadership
- 1 co-ordinator
- 4 game leaders who can help the participants when necessary.

4.2 Organisation
- The participants are divided into groups of 4 (the games can also be played with fewer participants per group).
- Each group receives a scoresheet.
- All tests must be done but the order is not fixed.
- The player in the group with the highest score receives 4 pts on the scoresheet. The player with the lowest score receives 1 pt (if there is a group with 3 participants, the player with the highest score receives 4, the second receives 3, the lowest score receives 2).
- When all the tests are done, give the scoresheet to the co-ordinator.
- The player with the highest score from the group is the winner.
- You can also determine a general winner.

4.3 Scoresheet

	Name	Name	Name	Name
Bell tossing				
Tin tossing				
Horseshoe tossing				
Petanque				
Stone tossing				
Shovelboard				
Skills circuit				
Cycling circuit				
Marbling				
Mini golf				
Pole jumping				
Tilt at the ring				
Beat the "see saw"				
Fishing				
Ball tossing				
Golf links				
Total				

4.4 Duration
Half a day.

5) Description of the games

5.1 Bell tossing
A bell is hung up in a hoop. From a 5 m distance each player tries to toss a ball through the hoop and to ring the bell when doing so. Each player has 5 balls. If each player has had a turn, everybody can try 5 more times. The best series counts.

scoring: Touching the bell = 10 pts
            Through the hoop without touching the bell = 5 pts.

(1 hoop, 1 bell, 5 tennis balls)

5.2 Tin tossing

On a table there are 10 tins stacked in a pyramid. From 3 m each player tries to knock over the tins with 3 balls. Each player has 2 tries. The best attempt counts.

scoring: Each fallen tin = 10 pts

(10 tins, 1 table, 3 tennis balls)

5.3 Horseshoe tossing

A 50 cm diameter circle is drawn round a pole. Each player has 5 horseshoes and from a distance of 5 m tries to toss the horseshoe as near as possible to the pole. Each player has 2 tries. The best series counts.

scoring: horseshoe completely around the pole = 50 pts
horseshoe in the circle = 25 pts
horseshoe on the circle edge = 10 pts

5.4 Petanque

Each player has 2 balls. The first player throws a small ball ("cochonnet") from behind the toss-line. The place where the small ball falls is the target for this game. The first player throws the first ball and tries to get it as near as possible to the target. Then the second player throws and then the third and the fourth. The player who is the farthest from the target throws the second ball and so on until all the players have thrown their second ball. The player whose ball is the nearest to the target at the end of the game gets 1 pt.
Then the second player throws the cochonnet and the game is played again. Repeat for the third and the fourth player.

scoring: Each player adds together their points for the four games.

(8 petanque balls, 1 cochonnet)

5.5 Stone tossing

5 hoops lie at a fixed distance from the players. Each hoop is worth a certain number of points. Each player has 5 stones and throws from behind the toss-line towards the hoops. The total number of points from the 5 stones are added together. Points are only given for each stone which lands completely in the hoop.

(5 stones, 5 hoops)

5.6 Shovelboard

Each player gets 3 turns to shove as many disks as possible into the gate (each gate has a fixed valve). After each turn continue playing with the disks which did not land in the gates. The winner is the player with the most points.

(1 shovelboard + disks)

5.7 Skills circuit

A 10 m x 10 m square is drawn on the floor. Each side of the square must be covered in a different manner by each participant:
- gunny sack running
- skipping
- moving sideways like a crab with a book on your head.

Each player starts with 200 pts and for every second the player needs to cover the circuit, 1 pt is deducted.

(chalk, gunny sack, skipping rope, book)

5.8 Cycling circuit

A circuit is laid out with cones. Each player tries to cover the circuit in the longest time possible (i.e., as slowly as possible). If a foot touches the ground or a wheel touches the line, then the time is stopped. Each second is worth 1 pt.

(12 cones, 1 bicycle)

5.9 Marbling

There is a hole 50 cm from the wall. The players stay behind a line 3 m from the wall and try to shoot a marble into the hole via the wall. Each player has 5 marbles and shoots 1 marble in turn. When everybody has shot all of the marbles, they are divided among the players again. Each marble in the hole is worth 1 pt. The marbles in the hole for both attempts are added together. If a player knocks your marble in the hole, you get 1 pt.

Variation: When playing in a hall, you can use a tray instead of a hole.
The tray must be open at the side of the wall.

(20 marbles, a half open tray)

5.10 Mini Golf

From a fixed place, the player will play the ball around the circuit and around obstacles, in as few strokes as possible. Each player starts with 200 pts. 10 pts are deducted for each stroke. The player with the most points at the end of the game is the winner.

(1 golfclub, 1 golf ball, 4 cones, 2 poles)

5.11 Pole jumping

On the field 10 circles are formed out of ropes about 1.5 m long. In a hall, circles are drawn with chalk. Each circle has a number. The distance increases more and more between circles. The player starts at circle 1 and jumps with a jumping-pole to circle 2, 3, etc. Each circle reached is worth 1 pt. When everybody has had a turn, start again. The best turn counts.

(10 ropes about 1.5 m in length, 1 jumping-pole)

5.12 Tilt at the ring

Rings are attached with clothes pegs to a clothes-line. Each player starts at the beginning of the clothes-line on a bicycle with a stick in hand. While cycling, they try to string as many rings as possible on the stick. The player is not allowed to stop. Fallen or dropped rings do not count. Each ring is worth 1 pt.

(10 x 5 cm rings, 10 clothes-pegs, 2 poles, 1 rope or clothes-line, 1 stick)

5.13 Beat the "see saw"

The player hits the highest end of a see saw with a stick, causing the ball to fly into the field. As soon as the ball has hit the board, the player runs into the field to catch the ball. If the ball falls, the player gets the number of points for that section. If the player catches the ball, the points are doubled.

(1 "see saw", 1 ball, 1 stick)

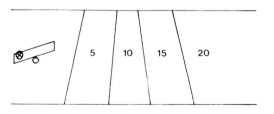

5.14 Fishing

In a hoop there are small blocks with rings attached. From a height (e.g., chair or box) the player tries to use a fishing pole (1 stick with string and a hook) to fish blocks out of the hoop in 1 minute. Each block is worth 1 pt.

(1 chair, 1 hoop, 1 stick + string + hook, 10 blocks with rings)

5.15 Ball tossing

3 buckets stand at a 4 m distance from the players. Each player tries to throw 2 tennis balls into each bucket. Everybody starts with 60 pts. 1 pt is deducted for each second that the player needs to throw the balls. If the tennis ball bounces out of the bucket, it is counted as good, but 3 pts are deducted.

(3 buckets, 10 tennis balls)

5.16 Golf links

Each player tries to hit a tennis ball through 4 gates with a hockey stick. The player starts at gate 1, where they must complete the last stroke too. You can only hit a non-moving ball. Each player starts with 16 pts. For each stroke 1 pt is deducted. The ball can enter the gate from the front as well as the back side.

(1 hockey stick, 1 tennis ball, 4 gates made out of cones)

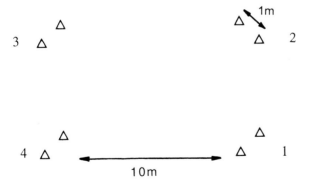

6) Organisational scheme

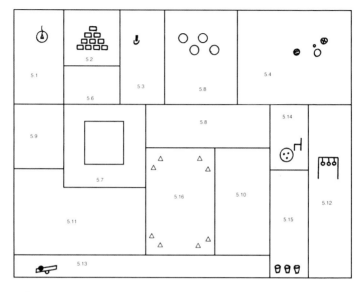

7) Equipment

- 10 tins
- 19 tennis balls
- 5 horseshoes
- 10 ropes (about 1.5 m in length)
- 4 little poles
- 1 cochonnet
- 1 shovelboard + disks
- 1 gunny sack
- 1 hook
- 28 cones
- 2 little poles
- 1 golf ball
- rope
- 10 clothes-pegs
- 1 "see saw"
- 10 blocks with rings
- 1 fishing pole (stick + string + hook)
- 1 hockey stick

- 1 table
- 1 pole (about 20 cm in length)
- 7 hoops
- 1 bell
- 8 petanque balls
- 5 stones
- chalk
- 1 skipping rope
- 2 bicycles
- 20 marbles
- 1 golf club
- jumping pole
- 10 rings (about 5 cm in diameter)
- 2 poles
- 12 tennis balls
- 1 chair
- 3 buckets

22. Living Cluedo

1) Activities and organisational form

Living Cluedo is based on the parlour game Cluedo. A murder has been committed and the players must try to find the murderer, the place of the murder and the weapon. To find the solution the participants must perform certain tasks by which they obtain information about the murder.

2) Location

Sports hall or open space.

3) Target group

- young people from 12-18
- can also be played by adults.

4) Practical organisation

4.1 Leadership
- 1 co-ordinator
- 1 game leader for the game board + distribution of information (i.e., police reports and newspaper reports about the murder)
- 6 game leaders for the tasks.

4.2 Organisation
- Groups of 4-6 persons.
- Each group has a pawn and a passport.
- At a central place you find the game leader with a large game board. The layout containing possible murder sites is represented on the board. The spaces between the sites are divided into 93 squares, each of which contains a task. When the groups arrive at a task, the game leader writes the task number on the passport and shows them the place where the task should be executed.
- The game tasks are devided into different categories. Each category is represented by a different colour. There are:
  - 15 technical exercises
  - 10 conditioning exercises

- 10 practical exercises
- 10 puzzles
- 5 rest stops
- 3 first aid tasks
- 13 theoretical questions (books can be consulted)
- 5 special tasks
- 12 cases without a task (e.g., return to where you were etc.).
- The game leaders for the tasks tell the groups what they have to do and sign the passports if a task is done correctly.
- When the groups arrive in a room, they receive an information sheet (police report, newspaper report, footprint, etc.) from the game leader. With this information the participants can attempt to solve the murder.
- Each group gets the same information in the same order.

4.3 Passport

Name of the group: ....
Pawn: ....

Murderer: ....
Weapon: ....
Place: ....

Task	Initial	Information sheet	Initial
		1.	
		2.	
		3.	
		4.	
		.....	

4.4 Duration
Half a day.

5) Game description

Each group chooses a name which is written on the passport and a pawn. Each group puts the pawn on a white square on the board. Somebody from the group throws the dice and moves the pawn the number of places equal to the throw. You can only move the pawn horizontally or vertically. When the group lands on a number, the game leader notes the number on the passport and the team executes the task corresponding to that number before moving on. When the group arrives in a room, it receives a form with details about the murder. You can only get into the rooms through the doors. When you have been through all the rooms, you have all the information about the murder. The group must find the solution to the murder as quickly as possible.

Note: You can work out the game in relation to the function of your groups

For example:
- school sport day
- murder place: class room
- possible murderer: teacher, director,...
- weapon: rope, cone, disk, etc.

6) Description of the games

6.1 Technical exercises

1. Shoot the ball 10 times into the basket.
   (1 korfball pole + basket, 1 soccer ball)
7. Knock over 10 tins (piled up in a pyramid) with a tennis ball.
   (10 tins, 8 tennis balls)
10. Break.
    (6 badminton rackets, 1 shuttlecock)
16. Slalom with a soccer ball between pins (4 players must each do this 1 time).
    (1 soccer ball, 8 cones)
22. 5 cones in a row: knock all the cones over with a soccer ball from a distance of 5 m.
    (1 soccer ball, 8 cones)

36. Throw 5 tennis balls into a bucket from a distance of 5 m.
    (5 tennis balls, 1 bucket)
38. Players stand in a circle: pass a volleyball 10 times underhand around the circle without interruption.
    (1 volleyball)
43. Players stand in a circle: pass a volleyball 20 times overarm around the circle without interruption.
    (1 volleyball)

52. From 10 m drive a tennis ball with a hockey stick and score (between 2 cones). Make 6 goals in total.
    (1 hockey stick, 1 tennis ball, 2 cones)
58. Bounce a table tennis ball upwards: the players' series are added together (count up to 200).
    (1 table tennis ball, 1 table tennis bat)
67. A circle is drawn on the wall: let the ten-
    nis ball bounce and then smash it
    into the circle (20 times).
    (1 tennis racket, 1 tennis ball)

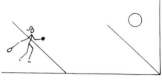

72. Divide the group in two. Stand across
    from each other: throw a basketball to
    the opposite side and follow the ball. Make 40 passes as quickly as possible.
    (1 basketball)
77. Juggle a ball keeping it in the air for 1 minute. If the ball touches the ground, the time is stopped. At the next attempt the seconds are added together, which gives the final score.
    (1 soccer ball)
84. There is a hoop hanging in a handball goal. From 5 m throw the ball 5 times through the hoop.
    (1 handball goal, 1 hoop, 1 handball, rope)
87. From 6 m, hit a tennis ball between two cones with a hockey stick.
    (1 hockey stick, 2 cones, 1 tennis ball)

6.2 Conditioning exercises

4. Skipping: 2 minutes.
17. 15 push-ups.
21. Arms stretched at shoulder height, 50 times hand pinching movements (the fingers are stretched open and shut).
39. 15 sit-ups.
42. 20 knee bends.
45. Stand with feet spread apart: alternate touching the left foot with the right hand and touching the right foot with the left hand.
61. 1 minute of cycling (supine position, legs high, hands support pelvis).
65. 1 minute of skipping.
81. By 2: sit down back to back and stand up 5 times.
88. From a high push-up position, jump to put the feet between the hands and then return to the push-up position.

6.3 Practical exercises

2. All stand in a circle and pass a tennis ball each time through your own swea-ter.
    (1 tennis ball)
12. Lie one behind the other and pass a ball with the feet.
    (1 volleyball)

25. Throw the ball backwards above the head. Bend forward and put stretched
    arms between the legs, catch the ball before it touches the ground.
    (1 volleyball)
44. Cover a fixed distance laid out with 6 pieces of cardboard without touching
    the ground.
    (6 pieces of cardboard)
46. Cover a fixed distance with a balloon between the knees. Take the balloon in
    hand, run back and pass it to the next player.
    (1 balloon)
51. Blow up a balloon until it explodes.
    (6 balloons)
68. Tie all the legs of the group together and cover a fixed distance.
    (rope, 2 poles)
70. Hold each others' hands and creep under a low hanging rope without letting
    go of each other.
    (rope)
76. Distance jump; the second player starts where the first landed, etc.
92. Pass a balloon from stomach to stomach.
    (1 balloon)

6.4 Creative tasks

11. Find an original cheer for the group.
15. Make a hockey stick and a ball from newspaper.
    (newspaper)
18. For 1 minute imitate "Mr Bean" (or another famous actor).
29. Each player must depict a sport in "slow motion".
53. Make up a spaghetti recipe without using the normal ingredients.
57. Create an advertisment about sporting gear.
60. Present a ballet sequence.
71. Sing and present the "elephant dance".
86. Mime playing basketball without a ball and without a basket.
89. Make a pyramid using the whole team.

6.5 Puzzles

At the numbers 5, 6, 8, 19, 28, 35, 62, 69, 78, 93, the team gets a puzzle which it has to solve as quickly as possible. Some possibilities are:

* Write a word, a sentence or a proverb in code.
    ex.   * A=1, B=2, ... Z=26
            19 16 15 18 20   19 19 8 15 = sports shoe

        * A=Z, B=Y, ... Z=A
        GL HDRN = to swim

* The next letter of the alphabet follows after each letter in a word. To decipher, you omit each second letter:
  BCABSTKLEFTUBCABLMLM = basketball

* Describe a word, a sentence or a proverb with a drawing (pictionary).

= goals

(paper, pencils, etc.)

6.6 Rest stops

3. Lie on the ground for 1 minute.
31. Sit in a yoga position for 1 minute.
40. Close your eyes for 1 minute.
64. Meditate for 1 minute.
83. Sit back to back for 1 minute.

6.7 First aid tasks

30. By 2: apply an elbow bandage.
    (bandage)
49. By 2: apply an ankle bandage.
    (bandage)
80. By 2: apply a head bandage (nose, mouth and eyes must not be covered).
    (bandage)

6.8 Theoretical tasks

When the team arrives on the squares numbered 9, 14, 23, 27, 33, 37, 41, 47, 55, 59, 85, 88 or 90, it gets a theoretical question about sport. Sport books may be consulted.

6.9 Special tasks

13. Each player must depict a proverb.
20. Each player must depict a profession.
56. Word parade: you make a combination of 50 words. The last letter of the first word is the first letter of the next word. All the words must have something to do with sport.
65. Take off your shoes. Find them blindfolded.
74. Unforeseen circumstances: The team must tell a story about a sport event. Each player can only say one sentence. The first player starts his sentence with A. The second goes on with B etc, till Z.

6.10 Free places (without tasks)

24, 26, 34, 48, 50, 54, 59, 66, 73, 75, 79.

7) Organisational scheme

dining-room			1	2	3	4	5	6	7	8	tent	
			9	10	11	12	13	14	15	16		
17	18	19	20	21	22	23	24	25	26	27	28	29
30	31	32	33	34	35	36	37	38	39	40	41	42
43	44	45	46	showers			47	48	49	50	51	52
53	54	55	56				57	58	59	60	61	62
63	64	65	66	67	68	69	70	71	72	73	74	75
tennis field		76	77	78	79	80	81	82	83	84	85	86
		87	88	stables		89	90	91	92	93	hall	

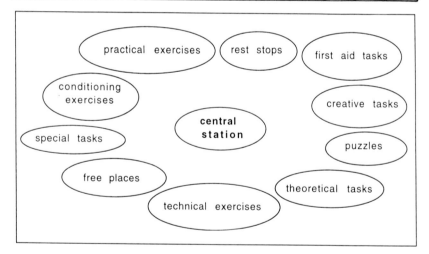

8) Equipment

- 7 blindfolds
- balloons
- 1 bucket

- passports for the teams
- foam dice
- a large board of the Cluedo game

- 1 small tennis ball
- 1 table tennis bat
- pawns
- books (theoretical questions)
- 14 tennis balls
- 4 hoops
- 10 tins
- newspapers
- 1 tennis racket
- 17 cones
- 1 skipping rope
- 6 pieces of cardboard
- paper and writing material

- duplicates of information papers
- bandages
- 1 korfball pole + basket
- 4 soccer balls
- 6 badminton rackets
- 1 shuttlecock
- 4 volleyballs
- 2 hockey sticks
- 1 basketball
- 1 handball
- 1 handball goal
- rope

23. Tennis Two to Twelve

1) Activities and organisational form

A combination of a tennis competition according to the tie-break rules and knowledge tasks.

2) Location

- Sports hall.

3) Target group

- young people from 12-18
- tennis players.

4) Practical organisation

4.1 Leadership
- 1 game leader.

4.2 Organisation
- Each tennis court is divided into 4 game courts (mini tennis).
- Some "thinking tasks" are posted around the tennis court (multiple choice questions).
- Each question has a number.
- The players answer the question and write the answer on a fill-in form where the question number appears.
- Then the player challenges another player for a game of tennis (tie-break). The team leader shows the winner of the game the place where the letter is to be filled in on the form.
- A second question is answered and a second player is challenged.
- The player has to find a word or a sentence as quickly as possible.

4.3 Fill-in form
found letters

1	2	3	4	5	6	7	8	9	10	11	12	13	14	15	16
...	...	...	...	...	...	...	...	...	...	...	...	...	...	...	...

correct place of the letters

1	2	3	4	5	6	7	8	9	10	11	12	13	14	15	16
...	...	...	...	...	...	...	...	...	...	...	...	...	...	...	...

word or sentence to find

1	2	3	4	5	6	7	8	9	10	11	12	13	14	15	16
...	...	...	...	...	...	...	...	...	...	...	...	...	...	...	...

4.4 Duration
Half a day.

5) Description of the multiple choice questions

All the multiple choice questions are in relation to tennis.

1) What is the most frequent injury among tennis players?
    - rheumatism in the toes: tennis toes (H)
    - knee inflammation: tennis knee (Z)
    - muscle inflammation in the arm: tennis elbow (E)
    - belly typhoid fever: tennis belly (N)
2) In official tennis competition is one allowed to use the following materials?
    - white or yellow foamballs (P)
    - foam balls of any particular colour (K)
    - white or yellow tennis balls (N)
    - tennis balls of any particular colour (S)
3) Does mixed tennis appear in official competition?
    - yes, in doubles and in singles (A)
    - no (C)
    - yes, only if the woman is 5 years older than the man (D)
    - yes, but only in doubles (B)
4) Which of the following is a Belgian tennis player?
    - Sabine Appelmans (U)
    - Mieke Vogels (A)
    - Steffi Graf (E)
    - Gerty Christoffels (I)
5) The dimensions of a tennis field for an official doubles game are:
    - 10.97 x 23.77 m (C)
    - 8.25 x 23.77 m (L)
    - 18.27 x 36.57 m (S)
    - 6.93 x 18.54 m (F)

6) In former years all tennis players used rackets with cords made of intestines. They were made of:
   - cat intestines   (H)
   - sheep intestines   (O)
   - human intestines   (W)
   - large intestines   (R)
7) Winning the game is possible with a score of:
   - 5 – 7   (A)
   - 5 – 8   (O)
   - 7 – 4   (I)
   - 7 – 5   (E)
8) What is this object used for? (photo of a ball thrower)
   - to pick up balls   (F)
   - to shoot balls   (M)
   - to recycle balls (grind old balls to make new ones)   (L)
   - to keep balls at the correct temperature   (Z)
9) Who is this? (Photo of Sampras)
   - Chang   (P)
   - Becker   (O)
   - Agassi   (A)
   - Sampras   (C)

10) If the ball touches the net on a serve and arrives in the right service zone, then it is :
   - deuce   (K)
   - let   (L)
   - lob   (N)
   -set   (D)

11) An underhand service is:
   - allowed   (O)
   - not allowed   (P)
   - only allowed in the lowest series (C 30)   (M)
   - only allowed in women's games   (L)

12) A ball returned in flight, before it touches the ground, is called:
   - overhead   (T)
   - drop shot   (F)
   - drive   (A)
   - volley   (L)

13) Player A "cuts" the ball over the net. The ball has so much backspin that it jumps back into A's court. B can not reach the ball, throws his racket at the ball and touches it. Racket and ball come over the net into the game field of A. A returns the ball, but out of the game field of B. This is:
   - the right act for B   (A)
   - error for B   (O)
   - let   (U)
   - error for A   (I)

14) In tennis is one allowed to jump during the service?
   - yes   (T)
   - no   (A)
   - yes, with both feet at the same time   (G)
   - yes, but not higher than 1 m   (K)

15) Which of the following matches is the most important and best known tournament played on grass?
   - Wimbledon   (R)
   - Roland Garros   (K)
   - Monte Carlo   (U)
   - Brussels   (N)

16) One of the players is missing something which the others have. Who?
   (photo of 4 tennis players on which one player does not have a wrist band)
   - player A   (S)
   - player B   (D)
   - player C   (O)
   - player D   (W)

The found letters are:

1	2	3	4	5	6	7	8	9	10	11	12	13	14	15	16
E	N	B	U	C	O	E	M	C	L	O	L	O	T	R	W

Correct place of the letters

1	2	3	4	5	6	7	8	9	10	11	12	13	14	15	16	17	18	19
W	E	L	C	O	M	E	/	T	O	/	O	U	R	/	C	L	U	B

6) Organisational scheme

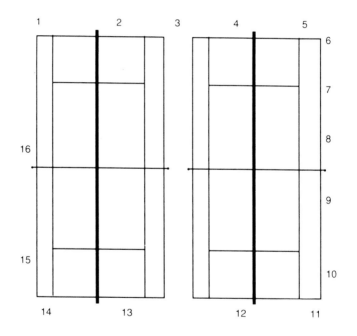

7) Equipment

- 8 movable nets
- 16 tennis rackets
- pencils
- tape

- 8 posts
- fill-in forms
- plastic covers containing the questions

24. Game without Frontiers

1) Activities and organisational form

Different teams compete against each other in a certain number of relay games.

2) Location

Soccer field or another open field.

3) Target group

- young people from 12-18
- adults
- the example is worked out for about 60 persons.

4) Practical organisation

4.1 Leadership
- 1 general co-ordinator
- 6 game leaders (1 per game).

4.2 Organisation
- The participants are divided into 6 teams.
- Each team has a team leader.
- For each relay game, the team leader and the team set up the equipment.
- After the game, the team prepares the equipment for the next game.
- Each game is demonstrated.
- The co-ordinator gives the start and the end signal.
- After each common game, a team plays the "fil rouge".
- The team leader is the referee for the team and pays attention to the way the team finishes.
- The co-ordinator fills in the scoreboard.

4.3 Scoresheet

Game	Team 1	Team 2	Team 3	Team 4	Team 5	Team 6
Bag racing						
Skippy ball						
Racing						
Korfball racing						
Balloon stroke						
Skill racing						
Towel volleyball						
"Fil rouge"						
Total						

4.4 Duration

About 2 hours.

5) Description of the games

5.1 Gunny sack racing

Each team is divided in groups of 3. The first 3 start at the starting line and have 2 gunny sacks. One player stands in each sack. The player in the middle puts a foot in the sack of each of the players beside her/him. At the starting signal, the players run to the cone, round it and return to the starting line. Here they pass the sacks to the next 3 players. Each team must complete the circuit 3 times.

scoring: The team that ends first gets 6 pts.
The team that ends last gets 1 pt.

(12 gunny sacks, 6 cones)

5.2 Skippy ball racing

Each team has 3 skippy balls which are connected with a piece of elastic. The first 3 players for each team sit on a skippy ball at the starting line. At the signal the players jump a slalom between the cones. After rounding the last cone, they return in a straight line to the start, where they pass the skippy ball to the next players. The circuit must be completed 3 times.

scoring: The team that ends first gets 6 pts.
The team that ends last gets 1 pt.

(18 skippy balls, 24 cones)

5.3 Korfball racing

Each player has a dice. The first player throws the dice. The number thrown is the number of goal attempts the player may undertake. After the player has thrown, they dribble the ball between the cones until they reach the basket where an attempt is made to score. If a goal is scored during the attempts, the player takes a letter and hangs it on a clothes-line. The player runs back with the ball and passes it to the next player.

scoring: The first team which forms the word "KORFBALL" gets 6 pts.
The team which last forms the word gets 1 pt.

(6 korfball poles + basket, 6 volleyballs, 24 cones, 6 clothes-lines, 48 clothes-pegs, 6 large dice)

5.4 Balloon stroke

Each 2 players have a balloon. At the starting signal a player from the first pair blows up the balloon and ties a knot in it. Both players slalom between the cones while keeping the balloon in the air. If the balloon falls, the team should restart at the previous cone. At the end of the circuit there is a chair. Here the players try to pop the balloon by sitting on it. When the balloon pops, they return hand in hand to the starting line. When they touch the second pair's hand, they can start to blow up their balloon.

scoring: The team that ends first gets 6 pts.
The team that ends last gets 1 pt.

(30 balloons, 30 cones, 6 chairs)

5.5 Skill racing

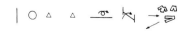

The first player for each team starts, runs to the hoop, picks up the hoop, pulls it over the body and puts it back in its place, runs to the cones, hops on one leg to the next cone, completes a forward roll on the mat, jumps over the rope and at the end, takes a piece of clothing which they put on. With the piece of clothing on, the player redoes the circuit in the reverse order. At the starting line, gives the piece of clothing to the next player. If they lose a piece of clothing, they must pick it up and put it back on.

scoring: The team that ends first gets 6 pts.
The team that ends last gets 1 pt.

(6 hoops, 12 cones, 6 mats, rope, 2 poles, 60 pieces of clothing)

5.6 Towel volleyball

Each team has 2 large towels. The players are divided into 2 groups. Each group has a towel and each player holds on to the towel. The team starts behind the line with a ball on top of the towels. By passing the ball from the towel to another, they try to put the ball into a tray (part of a box). If the ball lands in the tray, the ball is picked up and the team restarts at the starting line. Each team has to put 5 balls into the tray. If the ball falls on to the ground, restart at the place where the ball was last caught.

scoring: The team that ends first gets 6 pts.
The team that ends last gets 1 pt.

(12 towels, 6 volleyballs, 6 parts of the box)

5.7 "Fil Rouge"

Each player playing the "Fil Rouge" gets a tennis racket. At the starting line there is a bucket filled with water and some empty plastic cups. At the starting signal the players fill the cups with water, put them on the

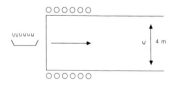

rackets, run to the other side and put the water in a bucket. At the same time, there are 2 players from the other team at the sidelines who throw foam balls at the runners. The places from where the opposing players may throw the balls are bordered by rope. The game lasts 3 minutes.

scoring: When all the teams have played the "Fil Rouge":
The team that puts the most water in the bucket gets 6 pts.
The team that puts the least water in the bucket gets 1 pt.

(10 tennis rackets, 6 buckets, 1 tray with water, plastic cups, 60 foam balls)

6) Organisation

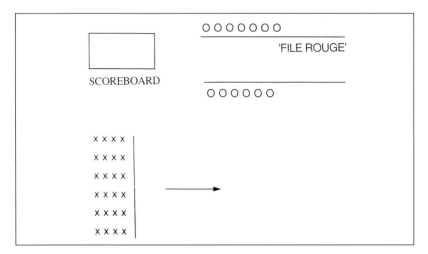

7) Equipment

- scoreboard
- whistle
- 2 poles
- 60 pieces of clothing
- 6 korfball poles + basket
- 6 volleyballs
- 42 clothes-pegs
- 1 box (6 parts)
- 10 tennis rackets
- 6 buckets
- 1 tray with water
- plastic cups
- paper
- 12 towels

- 60 foam balls
- rope
- tracing ribbon
- 12 buckets
- 6 boards
- 18 skippy balls
- 12 gunny sacks
- 30 cones
- 30 balloons
- 6 chairs
- 6 hoops
- 6 mats
- 6 large dice
- stopwatch

25. Gymnastics on a "Come and Go" Basis

1) Activities and organisational form

A number of gymnastic games are offered. The participants choose for themselves which games they will participate in, or they are cheered on or invited to do so by the organising staff.

2) Location

Sports hall.

3) Target group

- young people.

4) Practical organisation

4.1 Leadership
- 1 co-ordinator
- 2 persons responsible for the reception desk (showing people the changing rooms, giving directions, etc.)
- 8 game leaders (1 per game) wearing identical T-shirts.

4.2 Organisation

- The game leaders put the equipment in place.
- All the games have a big identifying name board.
- 15 minutes before the start of the games, one of the game leaders gives a general warm-up to music.
- Following the warm-up, all the game leaders go to their game and the games start.
- At the end of each game, one of the game leaders gives a general "cool down".
- The game leaders put the equipment away.

4.3 Duration

About 2 hours.

5) Description of the games

5.1 Large trampoline

Jumping, somersaults, falling on your back, falling on your stomach.

(1 large trampoline, 2 large mats, 10 small mats)

5.2 Horizontal bar

- Creep on to the box.
- Hang from the horizontal bar and move sideways.
- Climb up the bench to the top, jump over the horizontal bar on to a large thick mat.
- Do a "little turn forward" and a "little turn backward" on the horizontal bar.
- Step over the horizontal bar and go back to the box at the first horizontal bar.

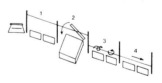

(2 parts of a box, 4 horizontal bars, 6 small mats, 1 large thick mat, 1 bench)

5.3 Long mat

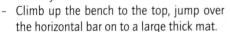
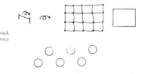

On the first part of the mat, do the sack race, then get out of the sack, throw it back, go over the rope, forward head roll, head roll with legs spread and creep under the net. On the last part, jump one foot into each of the 6 hoops – do this 5 times.

(1 long mat, 2 small poles + rope, 1 net, 1 large mat, 6 hoops)

5.4 Rings

Run, jump on to the jumping board, land on
the box on hands and feet, take the rings,
swing to the box, jump down from the box and start again.

(2 pair of rings, jumping board, 2 boxes, 4 thick mats)

5.5 Small trampoline

Run to and jump on to the small trampoline:
- as high as possible
- as far as possible
- over a stick
- to the ball
- "head" a ball during the jump
- float roll.

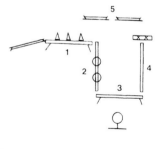

(1 small trampoline, 2 thick mats, 5 balls)

5.6 Balance beam

Run along the bench to the beam, run over
the first beam and step over the cone, walk to
the second beam, creep through the hoops,
walk to the third beam and throw a basketball into the hoop (someone stays at the hoop
to catch the ball and to pass it), walk backwards across the fourth beam to the middle,
turn and jump down at the end; run over the
overturned benches and run back to the first beam.

(4 balance beams, 3 benches, 3 cones, 3 hoops, 1 thick mat, 3 basketballs, 12
small mats)

5.7 Jumping

Run to and jump on to the jumping board,
over the vaulting horse, jump sideways over
the box, jump over the vaulting horse
positioned lengthwise, jump over 5 hurdles
with feet together, jump on the jumping board
and make a diving roll. Jump on the trampoline
and do a headroll on a high thick mat.

(2 jumping boards, 2 vaulting horses, 3 boxes, 5 hurdles, 2 thick mats, 1 small trampoline, 3 small mats)

5.8 Ropes

Climb on to the box, swing with the rope to the thick mat, walk down the bench, climb sideways on to the ropes to the box, stand up on the box, swing with the rope to the ball, kick the ball and score a goal, climb up the last rope, come back and then return to the first box.

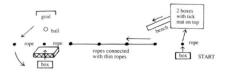

(7 climbing ropes, 1 long rope (to make the sideways connections) 4 boxes, 2 thick mats, 1 bench, 1 handball goal, 5 balls)

6) Organisation

small trampoline	ropes	balance beam	large trampoline
rings	horizontal bar	long mat	
		jumping	

7) Equipment

- 1 large trampoline
- 31 small mats
- 4 horizontal bars
- 1 long mat
- rope
- 12 hoops
- 3 jumping boards
- 10 plastic balls (beach balls)
- 3 cones
- 1 basketball hoop
- 3 basketballs
- music installation
- name board for the different games

- 12 thick mats
- 11 boxes
- 7 benches
- 2 poles
- long net
- 2 pairs of rings
- 2 small trampolines
- 4 balance beams
- 2 vaulting horses
- 5 hurdles
- 7 climbing ropes
- 1 handball goal

26. New Recreational Materials

1) Activities and organisational form

A variation of games with new recreational materials (a free choice programme). The participants choose the games they will perform or they are encouraged or invited by the game leaders to do so. They can try out new materials and use them afterwards in a game.

2) Location

Sports hall.

3) Target group

- children, but also adults may participate.

4) Practical organisation

4.1 Leadership
- 1 general co-ordinator
- 7 game leaders (1 game leader per 2 games)
  tasks: set up the material – supervision – encouragement
- all game leaders wear identical T-shirts.

4.2 Organisation
Alongside each game there is a sign with information about the game.
Take care that the activities are placed in such a way that:
- One activity does not disturb another.
- There should be space next to the activities to walk alongside or to observe.
- The whole set-up is visible.

Material
- The material must be clearly visible near the different games so that the participants see it as an invitation.
- The material must be:
  - inviting, colourful, of good quality
- Make an inventory of the materials used and give it to the game leaders so that all the materials are returned.

4.3 Duration
Half a day.

5 Description of the games

5.1 Fling-it

A fling-it net is a knotless nylon net with handles. Each net can be held by 2 or 4 persons.

By stretching and releasing the net one can play with a ball; specifically one can:
- throw a ball high and catch it again
- throw a ball from one to the other
- throw a ball into a goal
- etc.

By using balls of different size and weight the game can be made quicker or slower.

(4 fling-it nets, 4 foamballs, 4 balloon balls (= quicker than a balloon and slower than a foamball), 4 softballs, 4 tennis balls, 4 volleyballs)

5.2 Fling-it netball

The players are divided over the two halves of a volleyball court. On each side there are equal numbers of fling-it nets. The players divide the nets equally between them (2-4 players per net). Use volleyball rules.

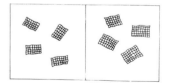

(8 fling-it nets, 1 tennis ball, 2 volleyball poles, 1 volleyball net)

5.3 Mono-fling

A mono-fling net is a 25 x 30.5 cm throwing net with handles. You can do the same exercises as with a fling-it net. The big difference is that everybody has their own net.

(8 mono-fling nets, 2 tennis balls, 2 foamballs, 2 balloon balls, 2 softballs)

5.4 Mono-fling game

The players are divided into 2 teams (minimum 2 players per team). Every player has a mono-fling net. The players pass the ball to each other and try to get the ball behind the rival's backline. The ball must be caught in the net of a player from one's own team before one can score 1 pt. The rivals try to intercept the ball.

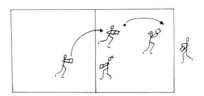

(12 mono-fling nets, 1 tennis ball)

5.5 Catch Ball

A Catch Ball has a vinyl centre with 6 coloured spokes. Each spoke has a different colour and a number. The Catch Ball is thrown to other teammates and one tries to:
- catch 1 spoke
- catch 2 spokes
- catch a defined colour
- catch 10 pts in as few turns as possible
- etc.

(8 Catch Balls)

5.6 Catch-baseball

A 15 x 15 m rectangle is marked out. On the corners, 4 bases are put. 10 m from one of the sidelines is the batter's box. Between the fault lines, 5 m from the plate, a tipline is drawn. Exactly in the middle between bases 1 and 4, is the pitcher's mound.

Rules of the game

One team is the batting team and is numbered. The other team consists of fielders which are positioned at the bases and at the pitcher's position (x). The field player at the pitcher's position throws a tennis ball underhand to the first batter. This batter strikes the tennis ball with a bat or a cudgel into the field and runs to bases 1, 2, 3 and 4. The field players try to catch the ball and throw it to the pitcher. When the pitcher has the ball and is on the pitcher's mound, the game stops. If the runner

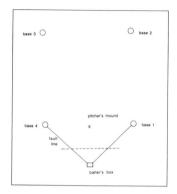

is not on a base at that moment, he/she is out. The runner may stop at any base. The batter must strike the ball over the tipline and inside the fault lines but as far as one can (you may hit further than bases 2 and 3). When each of the batting team has had a turn, the batting team becomes the field team. Each team has one turn.

scoring:

Each runner who arrives on base 4 without being caught "out" gets 4 pts (each base = 1 pt). The runner who makes a home run gets 8 pts.

(4 bases, bat, 1 tennis ball, 1 hoop)

5.7 Scatch

A scatch-set consists of 2 velcro-type catch boards and a velcro tennis ball.

Each player attaches the scatch board to their "catching hand". The ball is thrown back and forth (underhand or overhand) and is caught with the scatch board. The scatch board can also be attached to the ankle.

(10 scatch boards, 5 scatch balls)

5.8 Scatch hitball

The players are divided into 2 teams. Each team chooses a "king" who stays behind the backline of the opposing team. Each team tries to hit opposing players with the scatch ball. The players can avoid the ball by

catching it with the scatch board. The players that get hit, join the "king". The team which first touches all the players and the "king", is the winner.

(16 scatch boards, 1 scatch ball)

5.9 Zip-'n'-rip
Zip-'n'-rip consists of a yellow nylon band and a black nylon band with a nylon rope attached to it which has velcro on both ends. Two players put the bands around their waist and each one attaches one end of the rope to the band. This will rip off when too much tension is applied.
- One player tries to rip off the band (without using hands) and the other tries to prevent this.
- Both players start together and sprint to the other side, trying to outrun each other.
- "Twin touching": both players are linked together. They try to touch the other players without ripping off the band.

(5 zip-'n'-rip sets)

5.10 Zip-'n'-rip soccer
The players are connected in pairs with a zip-'n'-rip. The pairs are divided into teams. Each team has 2 goals on their half of the field. When the zip-'n'-rip band rips off, it must be fixed before the game continues.

(10 zip-'n'-rip sets, 8 traffic cones, 1 soccer ball)

5.11 Z-ball
The Z-ball is a full rubber ball with 6 bounce bumps. When the ball bounces, it changes direction very often.

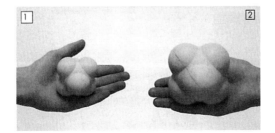

All kinds of throwing and catching exercises are possible:

- Throw towards each other while increasing the distance between each other.
- Throw towards each other while trying to make the Z-ball bounce as high as possible.
- Try to make the Z-ball bounce as much as possible.
- Etc.

(8 Z-balls)

5.12 Hoop Z-ball

The goal is a hoop which is fixed with a rope to the top of a pole.
The players are divided into 2 teams. Each team tries to throw the Z-ball through the hoop of the opposite team. The players are not allowed to run with the Z-ball.

(1 Z-ball, 2 poles, 2 hoops, rope)

5.13 CatchDisk

The CatchDisk is a soft frisbee, divided into 6 coloured and numbered sectors. The disk has to be thrown as an ordinary frisbee.

The coloured and numbered sections on the CatchDisk offer lots of possibilities:

- The players have to catch the disk with the thumb on top. The place where the thumb catches the disk determines the number of points. Play up to 20 pts.
- Each player chooses a colour. The disk is thrown to each other. Each time the disk is caught on a specific colour, the player with that colour gets 1 pt. Play up to 10 pts.
- Etc.

(5 CatchDisks)

5.14 CatchDisk frisbee

Play the game following frisbee rules (above). Only when scoring (this is when one receives a pass from a team mate in the goal area of the opponents) the team gets the number of points indicated by the thumb.

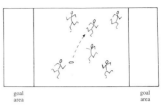

goal
area

goal
area

(1 CatchDisk)

6) Organisational scheme

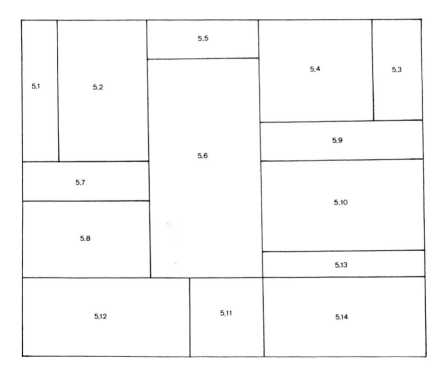

7) Equipment

- 12 fling-it nets
- 20 mono-fling nets
- 8 Catch Balls
- 6 foam ball
- 6 balloon balls
- 6 softballs
- 8 tennis balls
- 4 volleyballs
- 2 volleyball poles
- 1 volleyball net

- 26 scatch boards
- 6 scatch balls
- 15 zip-'n'-rip sets
- 8 cones
- 1 soccer ball
- 9 Z-balls
- 6 CatchDisks
- 2 poles
- 2 hoops
- rope

The Authors :

PAUL DE KNOP graduated in 1976 as licentiate in Physical Education from the Faculty of Physical Education of the Free University of Brussels, Belgium. Three years later, he obtained a second licentiate degree, namely in Leisure Agogics. In 1983, he obtained a Ph.D. in Physical Education at the same university with a thesis entitled "Study of a number of determining factors of efficient teacher behaviour during tennis initiation lessons". In 1997, he earned a Master Degree in Sports Sociology ans Sports Management from the University of Leicester (U.K.). His research interests lie in youth sport, particularly within the domains of sports sociology, sports pedagogy, and sports policy. He is also an active sports participant with a variety of interests and a number of certificates, such as in soccer (initiator – Royal Belgian Soccer Federation), tennis (Elementary Tennis Coaching Certificate – Great-Britain), skiing (initiator – French Ski School), volleyball, triathlon, windsurfing, running, swimming (Higher Lifeguard Degree – Flemish Trainers School), recreational sport (he is a recreational sports and swimming leader). He is also a recreational sports teacher (Dutch Sport Federation). He has organised several recreational sports events in Belgium and abroad. He is associate professor in the Faculty of Physical Education of the Free University of Brussels. His teaching includes areas of sport, leisure and physical education (organisational and policy aspects). He coordinates the research unit "Social Movement Agogics", the project "Elite Sport and Study" and the "Sport Management Committee" of the Free University of Brussels.

MARC THEEBOOM graduated in 1982 in Physical Education and in 1987 in Leisure Agogics from the Free University of Brussels. From 1984 to 1994, he was affiliated to this university as an assistant in the Faculty of Physical Education, where he was involved in teaching and research in sport, leisure and physical education. In 1994, he obtained a Ph.D. in Physical Education with a thesis entitled: "Towards the development of an alternative teaching programme for youngsters within the Chinese martial arts ('wushu')". Since then, he has been affiliated as an assistant professor and doctor-assistant in the Faculty of Physical Education. As a sports participant, he is actively involved in the Asian martial arts both as a teacher and international athlete. In 1997, he was appointed as Technical Director of martial arts of the Flemish Trainers School.

LINDA VAN PUYMBROECK graduated in 1985 in Physical Education and in 1986 in Leisure Agogics from the Free University of Brussels. From 1987 to 1996, she was affiliated to this university as an assistant in the Faculty of Physical

Education, where she was involved in teaching and research in sport, leisure and physical education. She has a wide sporting interest in volleyball, windsurfing (trainer B – Flemish Trainers School), ski (initiator – Flemish Trainers School), sailing (2nd degree – Flemish Trainers School), swimming (Lifeguard Degree – Flemish Trainers School) and recreational sport.

KRISTINE DE MARTELAER graduated in Physical Education from the State University in Ghent in 1988. In 1990, she graduated in Leisure Studies from the Free University of Brussels, with a thesis on "High level sport and study". Since 1989, she has worked as an assistant in the swimming department of the Faculty of Physical Education at the Free University of Brussels and since 1994 she has been the Technical Swimming Director of the Flemish Trainers School. In 1997, she obtained a Ph.D. in Physical Education with a thesis entitled: "Study of youth-centered organised swimming in Flanders". She has experience as a sports participant in judo, gymnastics, basketball and skiing.

HELENA WITTOCK graduated in Physical Education from the State University of Ghent in 1989. One year later, she graduated in Sports Management at the same University. Since 1991, she has been affiliated to the Faculty of Physical Education of the Free University of Brussels as an assistant, involved in teaching and research concerning sports management, event management and the organization of sports. Her research interests lie within the areas of sportsponsorship, strategic planning for sports federations and other management-related topics. She is an active participant of jazz-dance, modern dance, swimming and skiing.